Promise-Powered Prayers

How to Claim God's Promises

J. M. FARRO

ISBN-10: 1484918274

ISBN-13: 978-1484918272

Acknowledgements

I would like to take this opportunity to thank my husband, Joe, for helping me to put this project together, and for faithfully reading and editing my work on a regular basis. I could not devote myself to my ministry work without his constant support and understanding. He has been my best friend and confidant for more than 42 years.

I also sincerely appreciate my son, Joseph, and all of the valuable technical support and computer help he has given me over the years. His expertise, confidence, and calmness in stressful times have been a great inspiration and encouragement to me.

A special thanks to my son, John, who has allowed me to serve on the staff of his extraordinary ministry, Jesusfreakhideout.com, for the past 18 years. I am ever so grateful to him for telling me those many years ago, "Mom, you should write some devotionals for my site..."

Cover Photo by Amy DiBiase

How to Use This Book

The prayers and promises in this book are based on the Word of God, and because of that, they carry the authority and power of God Himself. Scripture says that there is "inherent power" in God's Word. (Colossians 1:6 AMP; 1 Thessalonians 1:5 AMP) So when we pray prayers filled with the Word of God, we open the door to divine intervention, and we close the door on the forces of darkness.

I pray many of these prayers over myself and my loved ones every day. I also pray many of them for my readers and my sisters and brothers in Christ around the world. Feel free to substitute "us" or "they" or "we" for "I" in these prayers. I have included confessions (declarations of faith), and actual biblical verses, as well as prayers. Allow the Holy Spirit to lead you in what and how to pray for yourself and others. And to make the most of this book, please read the following section entitled, "How to Claim God's Promises."

The second half of this book contains twenty devotionals that you can use daily or weekly. In this section, I share with you personal experiences and anecdotes that I hope will inspire, encourage, and challenge you.

The Bible talks about the "self-fulfilling power" of God's Word. (Isaiah 61:11 AMP) So God's promises carry His power to bring them to pass when we pray them in faith. May the Lord make Himself real to you, as you apply the prayers and principles in this book to your own life and the lives of others!

How to Claim God's Promises

"Pray to the Lord day and night for the fulfillment of His promises. Take no rest, all you who pray. Give the Lord no rest..." Isaiah 62:6 NLT

When you trusted Christ as your Savior and Lord, you inherited a wealth of divine promises. By believing and claiming these scriptural promises, you can live the abundant, victorious life that Jesus died for you to have. The Lord has given His children promises of provision, healing, wisdom, strength, peace, joy, and everything we need to fulfill our God-given purpose and potential on this earth. But these heavenly resources are not automatic; we have to lay hold of them by faith.

The Bible says, "Do not become sluggish, but imitate those who through faith and patience inherit the promises." (Hebrews 6:12 NKJV) Usually, before we see the promise come to pass that we are claiming, we will have to go through a period of patiently waiting on God. One reason why we don't see more Christians enjoying the rewards of God's promises, is that we have a tendency to lose faith before we receive the answer. We actually talk ourselves out of our blessings when they get delayed, by thinking, "I guess it just wasn't God's will." That may be true in some cases, but if we are walking in close fellowship with the Lord on a day-to-day basis – devoting ourselves to prayer and the study of His Word – we can trust that we are hearing from God when we ask for His will and wisdom in a situation.

Jesus said, "If you abide in Me, and My words abide in you, you will ask what you desire, and it shall be done for you." (John 15:7 NKJV) Why is it so important for us to be attuned to God's will in a situation? Because the Bible says that praying according to His will is an important key to answered prayer. "This is the confidence we have in approaching God: that if we ask anything according to His will, He hears us. And if we know that He hears us – whatever we ask – we know that we have what we asked of Him." (1 John 5:14-15 NIV) God's Word is God's will, so when we want to pray about something, turning to the Scriptures for guidance is the perfect place to start. That's why Psalm 119:105 (NLT) says: "Your Word is a lamp to guide my feet and a light for my path."

Let me give you some practical examples of how you can begin to claim God's promises for your needs. Suppose you need healing in your body. You can ask the Lord to lead you to some promises in His Word that cover your need. You discover Jeremiah 30:17 (NIV), which says, "I will restore you to health and heal your wounds." Then you begin praying, "Lord, I ask that You fulfill Your promise by restoring me to health and healing my wounds." If your healing is delayed, you can reaffirm your belief that God will act on your behalf by confessing repeatedly, "The Lord is restoring me to health, and He's healing my wounds!" And you can really delight the heart of God by beginning to thank Him in advance for fulfilling His promise to you by saying, "Thank You, Lord, for restoring my health and healing my wounds!" Notice how your faith increases, and your hope abounds, as you focus on the promise, instead of your circumstances. Over the years, I have seen my percentage of answered prayer increase dramatically, simply because I have decided to make my prayers promise-centered, instead of problem-centered.

Now suppose you have a material or financial need. You go to God's Word, and you discover that He has offered to be your provider as you put your trust in Him. You say: "Lord, Your Word says that You will liberally supply all of our needs, so I'm asking You to provide us with the money we need to pay our rent this month." (Philippians 4:19 AMP) When you want to pray for protection for yourself and your loved ones, you can say, "Lord, on the basis of Your Word, I ask that You give Your angels charge over us to guard us in all our ways." (Psalm 91:11 NIV) When I need specific guidance in a situation, I often say, "Lord, I claim Your promise which says that whenever I need wisdom, all I have to do is ask You for it in faith, and You will provide it generously." (James 1:5-6 NIV) Since Scripture says, "Put the Lord in remembrance of His promises," I sometimes pray: "Lord, I put You in remembrance of Your promise to make me abundantly prosperous in every work of my hand." (Isaiah 62:6 AMP; Deuteronomy 30:9 AMP) Are you eager to see God's plans and purposes for your life fulfilled? Then you can pray with confidence, "Lord, I ask that You fulfill Your purpose for my life, for it is written, 'The Lord will fulfill His purpose for me.'" (Psalm 138:8 NIV)

What are your personal needs today? Dig into God's Word, and begin claiming His powerful promises for your very own – then watch Him do what only He can do!

Lord, teach me how to abide in You and Your Word continually, so that I will always be attuned to Your perfect will. Help me to make my prayers promise-centered from now on, instead of problem-centered. Thank You that as I claim Your promises in faith, I will live the supernatural, abundant life that belongs to me in Christ!

Table of Contents

PART I

PRAYERS

The Armor of God

I have on the WHOLE armor of God. The Belt of Truth is buckled around my waist. My Breastplate of Righteousness is in place. My feet are fitted with the readiness that comes from the Gospel of Peace. I take up the Shield of Faith with which I extinguish every fiery dart of the evil one. I have on the Helmet of Salvation. And I take up the Sword of the Spirit, which is the WORD OF GOD! (Ephesians 6:13-17 NIV)

Our Authority in Christ

Lord, I thank You that You have given me power and authority to trample upon serpents and scorpions, and to overcome ALL the power of the enemy, and NOTHING shall in any way harm me! (Luke 10:19 AMP/NIV)

Thank You for giving me power and authority to cast out ALL demons, and to heal EVERY kind of sickness, disease, infirmity, and illness in Jesus' name! (Matthew 10:1 AMP; Luke 9:1 NLT)

Lord, thank You for giving me the keys of the Kingdom of Heaven, and whatever I BIND on earth will be bound in heaven, and whatever I LOOSE on earth will be loosed in Heaven! (Matthew 16:19 NIV)

Thank You that whatever I FORBID on earth will be forbidden in Heaven, Lord. And whatever I PERMIT on earth will be permitted in Heaven! (Matthew 18:18 NLT)

Lord, help me to take this seriously, as You have told me to – that a YES on earth is a YES in heaven, and a NO on earth is a NO in heaven. (Matthew 18:18 MSG)

Safety and Protection

Lord, on the basis of Your Word, I ask that You spread Your protection over me. Cover me, shelter me, and defend me – so that I may be filled with happiness and joy! (Psalm 5:11 NIV/AMP)

Keep me from all harm, Lord. Reveal Yourself to me as my Defender. Protect me day and night. Keep me from all evil and preserve my life. Keep Your eye upon me as I come and go, and guard me continually! (Psalm 121:7-8 NIV/TLB)

O Lord, be a wall of fire around me – protecting me from every enemy – and grant me Your radiant presence at all times. (Zechariah 2:5 AMP/MSG)

Give Your angels special charge over me to protect, defend, and guard me in all my ways. Thank You that Your angels will lift me up in their hands, so that I will never stumble or fall. (Psalm 91:11-12 AMP/MSG)

Because I fear and revere You, Lord – and because You have promised it in Your Word – I ask that You cause Your angels to set up a circle of protection around me day and night. (Psalm 34:7 AMP/MSG)

O Lord, bless me and surround me with Your favor as with a shield! (Psalm 5:12 NIV)

Strengthen and establish me; protect me from the evil one, and from ALL evil. (2 Thessalonians 3:3 NIV)

Rescue me from EVERY evil attack, Lord, and bring me safely to Your heavenly kingdom. To You be the glory forever and ever, amen! (2 Timothy 4:18 NIV)

O my God, stand at my side and give me strength. Deliver me from the lion's mouth! (2 Timothy 4:17 NIV)

Grant me the security, protection, and safety that give me hope, courage, and confidence. Let me lie down unafraid, and cause many to seek my favor. (Job 11:18-19 NLT)

Help me to follow Your wisdom, Lord, so that I may always live in safety and peace – untroubled and without fear of harm. (Proverbs 1:33 NIV/NLT)

Cause me to lie down and sleep in peace, and make me dwell in safety and confident trust, O Lord. (Proverbs 4:8 AMP)

I pray that NO weapon formed against me shall prosper, and that EVERY tongue that rises against me in judgment, I shall condemn and prove wrong. In the shelter of Your presence, hide me from the plots of people, O Lord, and keep me safe from accusing tongues. Thank You that peace, security, and triumph over opposition are my inheritance from You, and You will see to it that everything works out for my best! (Isaiah 54:17 AMP/MSG; Psalm 31:20 NIV)

"The name of the Lord is a strong fortress; the godly run to Him and are safe." (Proverbs 18:10 NLT)

"If you make the Lord Your refuge, if you make the Most High your shelter, no evil will conquer you; no plague will come near your home." (Psalm 91:9-10 NLT)

"Let the beloved of the Lord rest secure in Him, for He shields him all day long, and the one the Lord loves rests between His shoulders." (Deuteronomy 33:12 NIV)

Our Work

Dear Father, Son, and Holy Spirit, apart from You, I can do nothing (John 15:5 NIV), but through You, I can do all things. (Phil 4:13 NKJV) So I commit to You this day all of my ways, all of my works, all of my intentions, endeavors, and efforts, and I ask that You direct them, perfect them, bless them, anoint them, and crown them with success, in Jesus' name. (Proverbs 3:6 TLB; Psalm 138:8 NASB) And help me to enjoy and profit from every moment and aspect of them. (Ecclesiastes 5:19 NLT; Proverbs 14:23 NIV)

Lord, I roll all my works upon You this day – I commit and trust them wholly to You. Thank You that You will cause my thoughts to become agreeable to Your will, and so shall my plans be established and succeed. Lord, I commit all my ways to You – I trust also in You – and I thank You that You will bring them to pass. (Proverbs 16:3 AMP; Psalm 37:5 NASB)

O Lord, deliver and protect me from all forms of dread, especially the dread that leads to procrastination. Teach me how to rejoice in all of my labors, and to enjoy all of my work, even the most mundane and trivial tasks. Remind me that no matter what I'm doing, I'm actually working for You, and not for myself or others. Grant that my labor will find favor in the sight of God and man. And enable me to earn a good living doing what I love to do. In every endeavor, task, and undertaking, direct all my efforts and crown them with success! (Ecclesiastes 5:19 NLT; Colossians 3:23-24 NIV; Proverbs 3:6 TLB)

Help me to quickly carry out the tasks You have assigned me. Help me to never be lazy, Lord, but to always work hard and serve You enthusiastically. (John 9:4 NLT; Romans 12:11 NLT)

Lord, make me strong and courageous as I set about the work You've assigned to me. Don't let me be frightened by the size of the task, but remind me often that You are with me, and You will not forsake me. Thank You that You will see to it that everything is finished correctly! (1 Chronicles 28:20 TLB)

The Lord guarantees a blessing on everything I do, and He fills my storehouses to overflowing. The Lord blesses all the work I do. I lend to many and borrow from none. The Lord makes me the head and not the tail, and I am always on top and never at the bottom. I always have the upper hand! (Deuteronomy 28:8, 12, 13 NLT)

Bless all my skills, O Lord, and be pleased with the work of my hands! (Deuteronomy 33:11 NIV)

O Lord my God, show me Your approval and make my efforts successful. Yes, make my efforts successful! (Psalm 90:17 NLT)

I pray, Lord, on the basis of Your Word, that all of my work would bring me many blessings, benefits, and rewards! (Proverbs 12:14 NIV/TLB)

I thank You, Lord, that I am Your own handiwork, recreated in Christ Jesus, born anew, that I may do those good works which You predestined (planned beforehand) for me to do – taking paths which You prepared ahead of time that I should walk in them, LIVING THE GOOD LIFE which You prearranged and made ready for me to live! Hallelujah!
(Ephesians 2:10 AMP)

Dear God, teach me how to respectfully obey those I work for and with, always with an eye on obeying the real Master, Jesus. Help me not to just do what I have to do in order to get by, but help me to work with enthusiasm, as Christ's servant, doing what YOU want me to do. I pray that I would always work with a smile on my face, always keeping in mind that no matter who happens to be giving the orders, I'm really serving YOU. Remind me often that good work will get me good pay from my Master, Jesus! (Ephesians 6:5-8 MSG)

I can do my work only because Christ's mighty energy is at work within me! (Colossians 1:29 TLB)

May I always labor in such a way that You will endorse my work, declaring from Your throne that it is good! (Psalm 9:4 TLB)

Remind me often, Lord, that lazy people want much but get little, but those of us who work hard WILL prosper. (Proverbs 13:4 NLT)

I will be strong, I will keep up the good work, and I will NOT get discouraged, for my work WILL be rewarded. (2 Chronicles 15:7 NIV/TLB)

May the Lord reward my work, and may my wages be full from the Lord! (Ruth 2:12 NASB)

"But I said, 'I have labored to no purpose; I have spent my strength in vain and for nothing. Yet what is due me is in the Lord's hand, and my reward is with my God!'" (Isaiah 49:4 NIV)

I declare that I am steadfast, immovable, always excelling in the work of the Lord – always doing my best and doing more than is needed – being continually aware that my labor (even to the point of exhaustion) in the Lord is not futile nor wasted, nor is it ever without purpose. Hallelujah! (1 Corinthians 15:58 AMP)

Bless me in all my harvest and in all the work of my hands, and make my joy complete! (Deuteronomy 16:15 NIV)

Lord, open up new doors of opportunity for me that no one can shut, and send me divine connections that will help me to fulfill my God-given purpose and potential.

When new opportunities bring opposition, put me at ease, and remind me that You are always with me as I carry on with Your work. (Revelation 3:8 NIV; 1 Corinthians 16:9-10 AMP)

Cause me to excel in my work, Lord. Make me a skilled worker who is always in demand and admired, so that I won't take a backseat to anyone. (Proverbs 22:29 MSG)

When I am tempted to overwork, please bring to my remembrance Your Word which says that it is vain for me to rise up early, to retire late, to eat the bread of anxious labors – for You give blessings to Your beloved EVEN IN OUR SLEEP. I receive that, Lord, and I thank You for it! (Psalm 127:2 AMP)

Lord, I claim Your promise which says that You are NOT unjust – You will NOT forget my work and the love I have shown You as I have helped Your people and continue to help them. Enable me to show this same diligence to the very end, so that what I hope for may be fully realized. Don't let me become lazy, but empower me to imitate those who through faith and patience inherit ALL that You have promised! (Hebrews 6:10-12 NIV)

Help me to keep a clear mind in every situation, Lord. May I never be afraid of suffering for You. Teach me how to work at telling others the Good News, and to fully carry out the ministry You have given me.
(2 Timothy 4:5 NLT)

"Now, O God, strengthen my hands!" (Nehemiah 6:9 NASB)

Make me a hard and energetic worker, Lord. And guard me from laziness and idleness. Make my arms strong for my tasks. (Proverbs 31:17 NLT)

Lord, help me to always remember that You care about honesty in the workplace, and that MY business is YOUR business. (Proverbs 16:11 MSG)

Teach me to fear and reverence You, Lord, and to walk in obedience to You, so that I will eat the fruit of my labor, and blessings and prosperity will be mine! (Psalm 28:1-2 NIV)

Thank You, Lord, that I will NOT labor in vain – I will FULLY ENJOY the works of my hands! (Isaiah 65:22-23 NIV)

Thank You, Lord, that ALL of my hard work will profit me one way or another. (Proverbs 14:23 NIV)

Dear God, I ask that You comfort and encourage and strengthen my heart, and keep me steadfast and on course in every good work and word. (2 Thessalonians 2:17 AMP)

Help me to always do my very best, Lord, so that I will have the personal satisfaction of work well done, and I won't need to compare myself with anyone else. (Galatians 6:4 TLB)

Work in my heart, Lord, so that I am always prepared and willing to do any upright and honorable work that You send my way. (Titus 3:1 AMP)

Lord, I pray that I would always work hard according to Your will so that You can say to me, "Well done!" Make me a good workman who does not need to be ashamed when You examine my work. Help me to always know what Your Word says and means so that I can handle and teach it correctly. (2 Timothy 2:15 TLB)

"But my life is worth nothing to me unless I use it for finishing the work assigned me by the Lord Jesus – the work of telling others the Good News about the wonderful grace of God." (Acts 20:24 NLT)

Wisdom and Guidance

O Lord, grant me revelation from heaven, and help me to apply it to my own life, and to share it with others in life-changing ways. (Ephesians 1:17 AMP; James 1:5 NIV; James 1:22 NIV)

Speak to me, Lord, and help me to hear and to heed Your voice. (John 10:27 NASB)

Make me see and understand so that I know just what to do in every situation and circumstance. (Isaiah 28:26 TLB)

Make me sensitive and obedient to Your Spirit's leading in all things, so that I will always walk in Your perfect will, and receive Your absolute best! (Isaiah 1:19 NIV)

Lord, I offer You my body as a living sacrifice, holy and pleasing to You, as this is truly the way to worship You. I pray that I would never copy the behaviors and customs of this world, but that I would cooperate with You so that You could transform me into a new person by renewing my mind, and changing the way I think. Then I will learn to know Your will for me, which is always good and pleasing and perfect! (Romans 12:1-2 NIV/NLT)

On the basis of Your Word, Lord, guide me along the best pathway for my life. Advise me and watch over me. Don't let me be like a senseless horse or mule that needs a bit and bridle to keep it under control. Instead, give me a teachable spirit, a perfect heart, and a willing mind. (Psalm 32:8-9 NLT; Psalm 51:12 NIV)

O Lord, my God, teach me what is best for me, and direct me in the way I should go. Teach me how to live right and well. Show me what to do and where to go. Help me to pay attention to Your commands, to listen all along to what You tell me. Then shall my peace and prosperity flow like a river, with blessings rolling in like waves from the sea! (Isaiah 48:17-18 NIV/MSG)

Because You love to help me, Lord, I ask that You supply me generously with Your wisdom so that I know what You want me to do in every situation and circumstance. I ask boldly and believingly for Your guidance, without a second thought. And because I'm asking in faith, I DO expect You to give me a solid answer. (James 1:5-8 MSG/TLB)

Because I fear and reverence You, Lord, show me the right path to take every time; teach me how to always choose Your best. So shall I spend my days in prosperity, and I will live within Your circle of blessing! (Psalm 25:12-13 NLT/TLB)

I pray that if I ever leave Your paths and go astray, I will clearly hear Your voice saying, "No, this is the way – walk here," and I will quickly get back on course. (Isaiah 30:21 TLB)

O Lord my God, teach me what is best for me in every situation and circumstance, and direct me in the way I should go, so that I may always be in the center of Your will. (Isaiah 48:17 NIV)

Lord, guard me from trusting myself – which would make a fool out of me – and help me to constantly walk in wisdom so that I will be delivered and kept safe from all trouble and danger. (Proverbs 28:26 NIV/NASB)

Help me to always walk with the wise so that I can become wiser all the time. Guard me from companionships that will cause me to suffer harm. (Proverbs 13:20 NIV)

Lord, wake me each morning with the sound of Your loving voice; then shall I go to sleep each night trusting You. Point out the road I must travel; I'm all ears, all eyes before You! Save me from my enemies, for You are my only hope. Teach me how to live to please You, because You are my God. Lead me by Your blessed Spirit into cleared and level pastureland. In Your faithfulness and love, bring me out of all my distress and trouble! (Psalm 143:8-10 MSG/NLT)

Dear God, keep my days stable and secure – with salvation, wisdom, and knowledge in surplus – and remind me often that the key to this treasure is my reverence for You! (Isaiah 33:6 MSG/NIV)

O God, teach me how to live right and well. Show me what to do and where to go. (Isaiah 48:17 MSG)

Lord, help me to walk by Your Spirit continually so that I will not carry out the desires of the flesh – even where my eating and my drinking are concerned; even where my thinking, and my speaking, and my doing are concerned. (Galatians 5:16 NASB)

Dear God, the glorious Father of our Lord Jesus Christ, give me the wisdom to see clearly, and to really understand who Christ is and all that He has done for me. (Ephesians 1:16-17 TLB)

Lord, make me wise and understanding, and let me show it by my good life, by deeds done in the humility that comes from wisdom. Guard me from bitterness, jealousy, selfish ambition, boasting, and lying. Help me to remember that jealousy and selfishness are not your kind of wisdom, but that such things are earthly, unspiritual, and demonic. (James 3:13-14 NIV/NLT)

On the basis of Your Word, Lord, guide me along the best pathway for my life. Advise me and watch over me. Don't let me be like a senseless horse or mule that needs a bit and bridle to keep it under control. Instead, give me a teachable spirit, a perfect heart, and a willing mind. (Psalm 32:8-9 NLT; Psalm 51:12 NIV)

Help me to live a life that pleases You, Lord, so that You may give me the wisdom, knowledge, and happiness that You promise in Your Word. (Ecclesiastes 2:26 NIV)

Lord, "Your Word is a lamp to guide my feet and a light for my path" – so please help me to study, meditate on, and perform Your Word, so that I will always be in the right place at the right time. (Psalm 119:105 NLT)

God has united me with Jesus Christ. For my benefit, God made Him to be wisdom itself. Christ made me right with God; He made me pure and holy, and He freed me from sin! (1 Corinthians 1:30 NLT)

"Since You are my rock and my fortress, for the sake of Your name lead and guide me." (Psalm 31:3 NIV)

"But when He, the Spirit of truth, comes, He will guide you into all the truth. He will not speak on His own; He will speak only what He hears, and He will tell you what is yet to come." (John 16:13 NIV)

"For the Lord grants wisdom! From His mouth come knowledge and understanding. He grants a treasure of common sense to the honest. He is a shield to those who walk with integrity. He guards the paths of the just and protects those who are faithful to Him." (Proverbs 2:6-8 NLT)

Holiness/Sanctification

Lord, help me to make a clean break with everything that defiles or distracts me, both within and without. Make my entire life a fit and holy temple for the worship of God. (2 Corinthians 7:1 MSG)

Dear God of peace, sanctify me through and through, and separate me from profane things, and make me pure and wholly consecrated to God. May my spirit and soul and body be preserved sound and complete, and found blameless at the coming of our Lord Jesus Christ, the Messiah. Faithful is He Who is calling me to Himself, and utterly trustworthy, and He will do it!
(1 Thessalonians 5:23-24 AMP)

Dear God, grant me more and more of Your grace that teaches me to say "NO" to ungodliness and worldly passions, and that enables me to live a self-controlled, upright, and godly life in this present age, while I wait for the blessed hope – the appearing of the glory of our great God and Savior, Jesus Christ, who gave Himself for me to redeem me from all wickedness, and to purify me and make me His very own, eager to do what is good. (Titus 2:11-14 NIV)

"Create in me a new, clean heart, O God, filled with clean thoughts and right desires. Restore to me again the joy of Your salvation, and make me willing to obey You." (Psalm 51:10,12 TLB)

Lord, I take Your Word which says that You have begun a good work in me, and You will continue it until the day of Jesus Christ, developing that good work, and perfecting and bringing it to its full completion in me! (Philippians 1:6 AMP)

Help me to work hard to show the results of my salvation, Lord, obeying You with deep reverence and fear. For You are constantly working in me, giving me the DESIRE and the POWER to do what pleases You. Hallelujah! (Philippians 2:12-13 NLT)

"Search me, O God, and know my heart; test me and know my anxious thoughts. Point out anything in me that offends You, and lead me along the path of everlasting life." (Psalm 139:23-24 NLT)

O Lord, equip me with all I need for doing Your will, and produce in me, through the power of Jesus Christ, every good thing that is pleasing to You. All glory to You forever and ever! Amen! (Hebrews 13:21 NLT)

Lord, help me to keep myself pure so that I can be an instrument for special purposes – made holy, useful to You, and prepared to do any good work. I pray that I would run from anything that stimulates youthful lusts, and that I would pursue righteous living, faithfulness, love, and peace. May I always enjoy the companionship of those who call on You with pure hearts. (2 Timothy 2:21-22 NLT/NIV)

Cleanse me from my hidden faults. Keep me from deliberate sins! Don't let them control me. Then I will be free of guilt, and innocent of great sin. May the words of my mouth and the thoughts of my heart be pleasing to You, O Lord, my rock and my redeemer! (Psalm 19:12-14 NLT)

Help me to make every effort to live in peace with everyone, and to be holy, for "without holiness, no one will see the Lord." (Hebrews 12:14 NIV)

Lord, I thank You that You gave Yourself on my behalf so that You might redeem me from all iniquity, purchase my freedom, and purify me to be peculiarly Your own – eager and enthusiastic about living a life that is good and filled with beneficial deeds. (Titus 2:14 AMP)

Direct my footsteps according to Your word; let no sin rule over me. Do not let my heart be drawn to what is evil so that I take part in wicked deeds along with those who are evildoers. (Psalm 119:133 NIV; Psalm 141:4 NIV)

Lord, I am determined to live a blameless life with Your help – especially in my own home, where I long to act as I should. Help me to refuse the low and vulgar things; help me to despise all crooked deals of every kind, and to have no part in them. I will reject all selfishness and stay away from every evil. I will not tolerate anyone who secretly slanders his neighbors. I will not permit arrogance or pride. No one who practices deceit will dwell in my house; no one who speaks falsely will stand in my presence. I will make the godly of the land my heroes and invite them to my home. I will search for faithful people who are truly good to be my companions. And I will live my life for You in all I do! (Psalm 101:2-7 TLB/NIV)

O God, help me to make every effort to be found by You [at Your return] spotless and blameless, in peace [that is, inwardly calm with a sense of spiritual well-being and confidence, having lived a life of obedience to You]. (2 Peter 3:14 AMP)

O Lord my God, cleanse my heart, and the hearts of all my descendants, so that we will love You with all our hearts and souls, and so we may live! (Deuteronomy 30:6 NLT)

"The Lord will fulfill His purpose for me; Your love, O Lord, endures forever – do not abandon the works of Your hands." (Psalm 138:8 NIV)

"I'm not saying that I have this all together, that I have it made. But I am well on my way, reaching out for Christ, who has so wondrously reached out for me. Friends, don't get me wrong: By no means do I count myself an expert in all of this, but I've got my eye on the goal, where God is beckoning us onward – to Jesus. I'm off and running, and I'm not turning back." (Philippians 3:12-14 MSG)

"So let's keep focused on that goal, those of us who want everything God has for us. If any of you have something else in mind, something less than total commitment, God will clear your blurred vision – you'll see it yet! Now that we're on the right track, let's stay on it." (Philippians 3:15-16 MSG)

"And we all, who with unveiled faces contemplate the Lord's glory, are being transformed into His image with ever-increasing glory, which comes from the Lord, who is the Spirit." (2 Corinthians 3:18 NIV)

Battles and Conflicts

O Lord my God, I commit to You all of my battles this day. Fight them for me, Lord; win them for me; reveal Yourself to me as my Jehovah Nissi – my Banner, my Victory, and my Miracle! (Exodus 17:15 NIV)

I will not be afraid or discouraged, Lord, for the battle is not mine, but Yours! (2 Chronicles 20:15 NLT)

Thank You that I have You to help me, and to fight my battles for me. (2 Chronicles 32:8 NLT)

I praise You, Lord, that it is not by sword or spear that You save, for the battle belongs to You! (1 Samuel 17:47 NIV)

O Lord, You will fight for me, and I shall hold my peace and remain at rest. Hallelujah! (Exodus 14:14 AMP)

I rejoice that it is not by strength that one prevails, and that those who oppose the Lord will be shattered.
(1 Samuel 2:9-10 NIV)

It is written, Not by might, nor by power, but by My Spirit, says the Lord Almighty. I will succeed because of Your Spirit, Lord! (Zechariah 4:6 NIV/TLB)

"Give us aid against the enemy, for the help of man is worthless. With God we will gain the victory, and He will trample down our enemies." (Psalm 60:11-12 NIV)

"The very day I call for help, the tide of battle turns. My enemies flee! This one thing I know: God is for me!" (Psalm 56:9 TLB)

"The Lord is on my side, He will help me. Let those who hate me beware." (Psalm 118:7 TLB)

O Lord, oppose those who oppose me. Fight against those who fight against me. Put on Your armor, and take up Your shield. Prepare for battle, and come to my aid. Lift up Your spear and javelin against those who pursue me. Let me hear You say, "I will give you victory!" (Psalm 35:1-3 NLT)

Thank You, Lord, that real help and deliverance come from You! (Psalm 3:8 NIV/MSG)

Lord, I thank You that You are the One who goes with me to fight for me against my enemies to give me victory! (Deuteronomy 20:4 NIV)

I praise You, Lord, that even when many oppose me, You will rescue me unharmed from the battle waged against me. (Psalm 55:18 NIV)

"The Lord is with me like a mighty warrior; so my persecutors will stumble and not prevail." (Jeremiah 20:11 NIV)

O Lord my God, I commit myself to You. I put my trust in You. Make my innocence clear to everyone. Vindicate me, and make the justice of my cause shine like the noonday sun! (Psalm 37:5-6 TLB/NLT)

"The Lord is with me; He is my helper. I will look in triumph on my enemies." (Psalm 118:7 NIV)

I put on the whole armor of God so that I may be able to stand against the wiles of the devil. For I do not wrestle against flesh and blood, but against principalities, powers, the rulers of the darkness of this age, and spiritual hosts of wickedness in the heavenly places. I take up the whole armor of God, so that I may be able to withstand in the evil day, and having done all, to stand! (Ephesians 6:11-13 NKJV)

Though I walk in the flesh, I do not wage war according to the flesh. For the weapons of my warfare are not carnal, but mighty in God for pulling down strongholds. I cast down arguments and every high thing that exalts itself against the knowledge of God, and I bring every thought into captivity to the obedience of Christ.
(2 Corinthians 10:3-6 NKJV)

The Lord my God is with me. He is a mighty Savior. He will take delight in me with gladness. With His love, He will calm all my fears. He will rejoice over me with joyful songs. (Zephaniah 3:17 NLT)

"Our God will fight for us!" (Nehemiah 4:20 NIV)

Help in Times of Trouble

O Lord, You are my strength and my shield from every danger. I trust in You with all my heart! You help me, and my heart is filled with joy. I burst out in songs of thanksgiving! (Psalm 28:7 NLT)

O Lord, I am expecting You to rescue me again, so that once again I will see Your goodness to me here in the land of the living. I say to myself, "Don't be impatient! Wait for the Lord, and He will come and save you! Be brave, stouthearted, and courageous. Yes, wait and the Lord will help you!" Hallelujah! (Psalm 27:13-14 TLB)

Dear God, fulfill my desires because I reverence and trust You. Hear my cries for help and rescue me! (Psalm 145:19 TLB)

When I face many hardships and perplexing circumstances, Lord, rescue me from each and every one! (Psalm 34:19 AMP)

Stand ready to help me, Lord, because I have chosen to follow Your will. (Psalm 119:173 TLB)

My eyes are always looking to You for help, for You alone can rescue me. Come, Lord, and show me Your mercy, for I am helpless, overwhelmed, and in deep distress. Save me from all my problems! See my sorrows; feel my pain; forgive my sins, O Lord! (Psalm 25:15-18 TLB)

"I look to the Lord for help. I wait confidently for God to save me, and my God will certainly hear me." (Micah 7:7 NLT)

O Lord, You will never let me down. You will never look the other way when I am being kicked around. You won't wander off to do Your own thing. You are always right here, listening to me! (Psalm 22:24 MSG)

Lord, even to my old age and gray hairs, sustain me. You have made me, so carry me, sustain me, and rescue me according to Your Word! (Isaiah 46:4 NIV)

Lord, I thank You that You have promised to hear me when I call to You for help. Rescue me from all my troubles. Let me feel You close to me when I am brokenhearted. Rescue me when I am crushed in spirit. (Psalm 34:17-18 NLT)

"Surely God is my help; the Lord is the One who sustains me." (Psalm 54:4 NIV)

"O Lord, from the depths of despair I cry for Your help: 'Hear me! Answer! Help me!' Lord, if You keep in mind our sins, then who can ever get an answer to his prayers? But You forgive! What an awesome thing this is! That is why I wait expectantly, trusting God to help, for He has promised." (Psalm 130:1-5 TLB)

Oh Lord, I praise You that You have not forgotten how to help me. You are not so decrepit that You can't deliver me. You are as powerful as ever! (Isaiah 50:2 MSG)

God is my refuge and strength, always ready to help me in times of trouble. Therefore, I will not fear! (Psalm 46:1 NLT)

If I am attacked and knocked down, I will know that there is Someone who will lift me up again. Yes, the Lord will save me! (Job 22:29 TLB)

Where does my help come from? My help comes from the Lord, the Maker of Heaven and earth. He will not let my foot slip. He who watches over me will not slumber or sleep. (Psalm 121:1-3 NIV)

"Because the Sovereign Lord helps me, I will not be disgraced. Therefore, I have set my face like a stone, determined to do His will. And I know that I will not be put to shame. He who gives me justice is near." (Isaiah 50:7-8 NLT)

"Great is the Lord, who enjoys helping His servant." (Psalm 35:27 NLT)

"Please, God, rescue me! Come quickly, Lord, and help me." (Psalm 70:1 NLT)

"My eyes are ever looking to the Lord for help, for He alone can rescue me." (Psalm 25:15 TLB)

"Summon Your power, O God; show us Your strength, O God, as You have done before." (Psalm 68:28 NIV)

"Please hurry to my aid, O God. You are my helper and my Savior; O Lord, do not delay." (Psalm 70:5 NLT)

"I will keep on hoping for Your help; I will praise You more and more." (Psalm 71:14 NLT)

"I was pushed back and about to fall, but the Lord helped me. The Lord is my strength and my defense; He has become my salvation." (Psalm 118:13-14 NIV)

"Be kind to me, God; I've been kicked around long enough. Once You've pulled me back from the gates of death, I'll write the book on Hallelujahs; on the corner of Main and First I'll hold a street meeting; I'll be the song leader; we'll fill the air with salvation songs." (Psalm 9:13-14 MSG)

"God takes the side of the helpless; when I was at the end of my rope, He saved me." (Psalm 116:6 MSG)

"God proves to be good to the man who passionately waits, to the woman who diligently seeks. It's a good thing to quietly hope, quietly hope for help from God." (Lamentations 3:25-26 MSG)

O Lord, You will defend and protect and avenge me, Your chosen one, when I cry to You day and night. You will not delay help on my behalf, but You will defend and protect and avenge me speedily! (Luke 18:7-8 AMP)

The Lord rescues the godly! He is my fortress in times of trouble. He helps me, rescuing me from the wicked. He saves me and I find shelter in Him! (Psalm 37:39-40 NLT)

"You, O God, do see trouble and grief; You consider it to take it in hand. The victim commits himself to You; You are the helper of the fatherless." (Psalm 10:14 NIV)

Thank You, Lord, that You are concerned for me, and You will come to help me! (Ezekiel 36:9 NLT)

"We depend upon the Lord alone to save us. Only He can help us; He protects us like a shield. No wonder we are happy in the Lord! For we are trusting Him. We trust His holy name. Yes, Lord, let Your constant love surround us, for our hopes are in You alone." (Psalm 33:20-22 TLB)

Deliverance and Healing

Dear Heavenly Father, nothing is impossible with You. (Luke 1:37 NASB) Nothing is too difficult for You. (Jeremiah 32:27 NASB) Nothing can hinder You. (1 Samuel 14:6 NIV) You can heal every kind of sickness, disease, infirmity, pain, and symptom – every kind of wound and injury – every imbalance and deficiency of the body. And You have promised to be my Healer. (Exodus 15:26 NASB) Therefore, I ask that right now, You cause Your healing power to flow mightily throughout every part of my body, throughout every fiber of my being, so that my health and healing will spring forth speedily at a supernatural rate – and so that I will be delivered and protected from every ailment, affliction, pain, symptom, and sorrow from this moment on, in Jesus' name. (Isaiah 58:8 NKJV)

Satan, I bind you and all the forces of evil, and I make You powerless to operate against me in any way, in the name and authority of the Lord Jesus Christ, the Holy One of God. Sickness, disease, infirmity, and pain – wounds, injuries, and symptoms of every kind – I rebuke you at your source, and I command you to loose me and let me go free now and forever, in the name of Jesus of Nazareth. (Matthew 18:18 NASB) I command every organ, every tissue, and every cell of my body – every system in my body – to come into line with the Word of God, and with the finished work of Christ on the Cross, and be healed and made whole right now, in the name of Jesus. (Isaiah 53:5 NKJV; John 19:30 NASB)

I declare that the same Spirit that raised Christ from the dead lives in me, and gives life and health to my mortal body, every moment of every day. (Romans 8:11 NIV) I am saved, healed, and made whole by the precious Blood of the Lamb of God! Thank You, Lord, for giving me power and authority to heal every disease, sickness, and symptom in the name of Jesus Christ – the name above every name! (Matthew 10:1 NASB; Philippians 2:9 NASB) Amen and amen!

Healing Promise Prayers

Lord, lead me along Your perfect pathway of healing and wholeness, and help me to follow You closely, and cooperate with You fully and joyfully all the way. Make Yourself real to me now in healing, comforting, and life-changing ways. Help me to always seek first Your kingdom and Your righteousness, so that all these things – even perfect health and wholeness – will be given to me as well! (John 14:21 AMP; Matthew 6:33 NIV)

Lord, I thank You that You have promised to be my Healer. Bless my food and water, and remove all sickness from me, and give me a long, full life. (Exodus 15:26 NASB; Exodus 23:25-26 NASB/NIV)

Keep me free from EVERY disease, according to Your Word. (Deuteronomy 7:15 NIV)

Bring me health and healing, Lord, and let me enjoy an abundance of peace, prosperity, security, stability, and truth. (Jeremiah 33:6 AMP/NIV)

Lord, fill my mouth with words to soothe and heal myself and others. (Proverbs 12:18 TLB)

Give me a happy heart that does me good like a medicine, and a cheerful mind that works healing. Guard me from the gloom and doom that can leave me bone-tired, and from a broken spirit that can sap my strength and make me sick. (Proverbs 17:22 AMP/MSG)

Jesus, Son of David, have mercy on me! I believe that You are willing and able to heal me. According to my faith, let it be done to me! (Matthew 9:27-30 NASB; Matthew 8:2-3 NASB)

Dear God, make my light break forth like the dawn; make my healing quickly appear; cause my godliness to be a shield before me; let the glory of the Lord protect me from behind. (Isaiah 58:8 NIV/TLB)

When I am sick or suffering, nurse me back to health, and ease my pain and discomfort, Lord. (Psalm 41:3 NLT)

"Heal me, O Lord, and I shall be healed; save me, and I shall be saved, for You are my praise." (Jeremiah 17:14 NKJV)

Teach me to pay attention to Your words, Lord, and to listen to Your sayings. Help me to keep them before my eyes, and deep within my heart. Then they will be life to me, and health to my whole body. (Proverbs 4:20-22 NASB)

I call upon every part of my body, and every fiber of my being to praise the Lord! May I never forget the good things He does for me. He forgives ALL my sins, and He heals ALL of my diseases. Praise His Holy name! (Psalm 103:2-3 NLT)

I cry out to You in my time of trouble, dear Lord, and I ask that You deliver me from all my distresses. Send forth Your Word and heal me; rescue me from every pit, and from every form of destruction. (Psalm 107:19-20 AMP)

Help me to never forget Your commands, Lord, because You use them to restore my joy and health. (Psalm 119:93 NLT)

Don't let me be impressed with my own wisdom. Instead, help me to fear and reverence You, and to turn away from all evil. Then I will have healing for my body and strength for my bones. (Proverbs 3:5-8 NLT)

Dear God, restore me to health and heal my wounds, just like You have promised in Your Word. (Jeremiah 30:17 NIV)

Because I fear and reverence Your name, O Lord, cause the Sun of Righteousness to shower me with healing from His wings. Then I shall go free, leaping with joy like a calf let out to pasture. (Malachi 4:2 NLT)

O Lord, guide me continually; satisfy me with all good things. Strengthen my frame and make my bones strong. Restore my strength, and keep me healthy, too. Make me like a well-watered garden, like an ever-flowing spring. (Isaiah 58:11 NIV/TLB)

"O Lord, Your discipline is good and leads to life and health. Oh, heal me and make me live!" (Isaiah 38:16 TLB)

"I shall not die, but live, and declare the works of the Lord." (Psalm 118:17 NKJV)

Lord, Your Word says that the prayer of faith will make me well, and if I have sinned, I will be forgiven. So, on the basis of my faith in You and Your promise, I ask that You raise me up, restore me to health, and forgive my sins, in Jesus' name. (James 5:14-16 NIV)

I pray that I would prosper in every way, and that my body would keep well, even as my soul keeps well and prospers. (3 John 2 AMP)

May the God of peace Himself sanctify me through and through, and separate me from profane things, and make me pure and wholly consecrated to God. And may my spirit and soul and body be preserved SOUND AND COMPLETE, and found blameless at the coming of our Lord Jesus Christ, the Messiah. Faithful is He Who is calling me to Himself, and utterly trustworthy, and He will do it! (1 Thessalonians 5:23-24 AMP)

Grant me a strong spirit that sustains me in bodily pain or trouble, Lord, and guard me from a weak and broken spirit. (Proverbs 18:14 AMP)

Dear God, heal my broken heart, bind up my wounds, and cure my pains and sorrows. (Psalm 147:3 AMP)

Lord, remember Your promise to guard the feet of Your faithful ones, and please guard my feet from all pain, disease, and injury. (1 Samuel 2:9 NIV)

Thank You, Lord, that You bore my griefs, sicknesses, weaknesses, and distresses; You carried my sorrows and pains. You were wounded for my transgressions; You were bruised for my guilt and iniquities. You received the chastisement needed to obtain peace and well-being for me. And with the stripes that wounded You, I am healed and made whole! (Isaiah 53:4-5 AMP)

You, Lord, bore my sins in Your own body on the Cross, so that I could die to sin and live for righteousness. By Your wounds I have been healed! Hallelujah! (1 Peter 2:24 NIV)

Dear Lord, I thank You that in order to fulfill what was spoken through Isaiah the prophet, You took up my infirmities and carried away my diseases. Glory to God forevermore! (Matthew 8:16-17 NASB)

"O Lord my God, I cried to You for help, and You healed me. O Lord my God, I will give thanks to You forever." (Psalm 30:2,12 NASB)

Healing Confessions

When you take medications, pray: Lord, I commit these medications to You, and I ask that You bless, anoint, and energize them, and use them to bring speedy, complete, and permanent healing to my body, in Jesus' name.

Lord, I thank You that You are my Healer. I commit myself to You, along with all of my healing needs. I receive all the healing You have for me this day: I take it into every part of my body, into every fiber of my being, into every area of my life – and I give You the thanks and the praise for it all, in Jesus' name! (Exodus 15:26 NASB; Philippians 4:19 NIV)

Jesus, I make You Lord over every area of my life – spirit, soul, and body. I claim You as my Healer. Sickness, disease, infirmity, and pain shall no longer lord it over me – Jesus is my Lord!

Thank You, Lord, that the healing power of God is working mightily in every part of me right now. Thank You that You are restoring me to health and wholeness. (Jeremiah 30:17 NIV)

My faith in Jesus heals me and makes me whole. (Matthew 9:22 NIV/KJV)

Jesus Christ the Messiah NOW makes me whole! (Acts 9:34 AMP)

It is the name of Jesus Christ, and my faith in His name – the faith that comes through Him – that gives me complete healing and perfect health. (Acts 3:16 NIV/TLB)

It is by the name of Jesus Christ of Nazareth – who was crucified, and whom God raised from the dead – that I stand healed and whole! (Acts 4:10 NIV/KJV)

I am the righteousness of God in Christ Jesus, and by His stripes, I am healed and made whole! (2 Corinthians 5:21 NIV; 1 Peter 2:24 NKJV)

Lord, I declare that You are my Divine Physician and my Healer. I believe and say that Your healing power is working mightily in every part of me right now. My health is springing forth speedily. My healing is quickly appearing. Thank You that the same Spirit that raised Christ from the dead lives in me, and gives life and health to my mortal body every moment of every day! (Exodus 15:26 NASB; Isaiah 58:8 KJV/NIV; Romans 8:11 NIV)

Lord, I thank You that this [name affliction or symptom] is NOT from You. Therefore, I reject it, I rebuke it, and I command it to leave my body now and forever, in Jesus' name! (Mark 11:23 NIV)

I'm not having you, [name affliction]! You are not of God, and I'm not having you! You get out of my body! You get out of my house! I resist you, I rebuke you, in Jesus' name! (Mark 11:23 NIV; James 4:7 NIV)

Thank You, Lord, for keeping me free from EVERY disease – even from [name disease, affliction, or symptom]! (Deuteronomy 7:15 NIV)

The Lord will make an utter end of [name affliction] for me, and affliction shall NOT rise up a second time! (Nahum 1:9 NKJV)

Lord, I thank You that every trace of [name affliction] is leaving my body right now, never to return, in Jesus' name!

Lord, I receive healing for my [name body part] in Jesus' name!

I take this very seriously: A 'yes' on earth is a 'yes' in heaven; a 'no' on earth is a 'no' in heaven. (Matthew 18:18 MSG) Therefore, I say NO to [name affliction] in my body. In the name of Jesus Christ I say NO!

Prosperity and Provision

Lord, I thank You that You make it clear in Your Word that You have plans to prosper me, and not to harm me – plans to give me hope and a future. Therefore, I declare that God is good, and His plans for me are good! (Jeremiah 29:11 NIV)

Dear God, on the basis of Your Word, I ask that You help me to make it my ambition to lead a quiet life, to mind my own business, and to work with my hands, so that my daily life may win the respect of outsiders, and so that I will not be dependent on anyone – being self-supporting, and having need of nothing!
(1 Thessalonians 4:11 NIV/AMP)

O Lord my God, teach me to profit, and lead me in the way I should go. (Isaiah 48:17 NASB)

I magnify You, Lord, because You delight and take pleasure in the prosperity of Your servant! (Psalm 35:27 AMP)

O Lord, give me Your blessing that brings me wealth without painful toil for it. (Proverbs 10:22 NIV)

Make me abundantly prosperous in everything I do, according to Your Word, Lord. (Deuteronomy 30:9 AMP)

Teach me how to pursue righteousness and love, so that I will find the life, prosperity, and honor that You promise in Your Word. (Proverbs 21:21 NIV)

I stand on Your Word which says that You will liberally supply and fill to the full my every need according to Your riches in glory in Christ Jesus. Hallelujah! (Philippians 4:19 AMP)

I claim Your promise, Lord, which says that You will give me food and provision because I reverence and worship You, and You will remember Your covenant forever, and imprint it on Your mind. (Psalm 111:5 AMP)

Make me rich in every way, so that I can be generous on every occasion. (2 Corinthians 9:11 NIV)

Lord, You provide seed for the sower and bread for food, so I ask that You provide and multiply my seed – that is, my resources – and increase the harvest of my righteousness! (2 Corinthians 9:10 AMP)

"Remember me, Lord, when You show favor to Your people, come to my aid when You save them, that I may enjoy the prosperity of Your chosen ones." (Psalm 106:4-5 NIV)

I take Your Word which says that I will not be disgraced in hard times, and even in famine, I will have more than enough! (Psalm 37:19 NLT)

Remember Your promise which says that ALL of my hard work shall profit me! (Proverbs 14:23 NIV)

Thank You, Lord, that because You are my Shepherd, You will continually feed, guide, and shield me, and I shall not lack! (Psalm 23:1 AMP)

On the basis of Your Word, Lord, I declare that wealth and riches are in my house, and my righteousness endures forever! (Psalm 112:3 NIV)

I claim Your promise which says that the worker deserves his wages. Hallelujah! (Luke 10:7 NIV)

Lord, I take Your Word which says that I will always have plenty to eat, until I am full, and I will praise Your name because You work miracles for me! (Joel 2:26 NIV/NLT)

Give me honor and praise among all people, Lord, and restore my fortunes before my very eyes. (Zephaniah 3:20 NIV)

Bring me out of every bondage, into prosperity, for You are true to Your Word. (Psalm 68:6 NKJV)

O Lord, I choose You as my Sun and Shield. Bestow favor and honor upon me. Do not withhold any good thing from me, and make my walk blameless before You. (Psalm 84:11 NIV)

I claim Your promise which says that You will make me prosper more than ever before! (Ezekiel 36:11 NIV)

Thank You for Your promise, Lord, which says that prosperity is the reward of the righteous. Hallelujah! (Proverbs 13:21 NIV)

I stand upon Your Word which says that the house of the righteous contains great treasure. (Proverbs 15:6 NIV)

Lord, I long to live a long and prosperous life, so help me to keep my tongue from speaking evil, and my lips from telling lies. (Psalm 34:12-13 NLT)

Remember Your promise to repay me two blessings for each of my troubles, Lord, and to restore double my former prosperity to me. (Zechariah 9:12 NLT/AMP)

On the basis of Your Word, Lord, I declare, "The God of heaven Himself will prosper us!" (Nehemiah 2:20 NKJV)

O Lord my God, increase me a thousand times, and bless me as You have promised! (Deuteronomy 1:11 NIV)

Help me to study Your Word continually, Lord. Lead me to meditate on it day and night, and to be sure to obey everything written in it. Then I will prosper and succeed in all I do, just like You promised. (Joshua 1:8 NLT)

I pray that my future will be so prosperous that my beginnings will seem humble! (Job 8:7 NIV)

I take Your Word, Lord, which says that as long as I seek guidance from You and follow Your paths, You will bless me and prosper me! (2 Chronicles 26:5 NLT/TLB)

O Lord, help me to trust in Your provision at all times, so that I can flourish like leaves in the springtime – and guard me from trusting in riches, which will cause me to fall and fail. (Proverbs 11:28 AMP/NLT)

Lord, make me generous and a source of blessing to others, for then I shall be prosperous and enriched, according to Your Word. By Your grace, I will refresh others, and I will reap the refreshment and generosity I have sown. (Proverbs 11:25 AMP/NIV)

I choose to yield and submit myself to You, Lord, and to agree with You and be conformed to Your will – so shall I have peace and prosperity, and great good will come to me! (Job 22:21 AMP)

O Lord, make me increase more and more – me and my children! (Psalm 115:14 NKJV)

Don't ever let me forget that You are the One who gives me the ability and power to produce wealth, Lord. (Deuteronomy 8:18 NIV)

Make me a faithful, trustworthy person who will be richly blessed, and guard me from an eagerness to get rich that will not go unpunished. (Proverbs 28:20 NIV)

Dear God, I pray that I would never be arrogant, and that I would never put my hope in wealth, which is so uncertain. Instead, I pray that I would always put my hope in You, because You richly provide me with everything for my enjoyment. Help me to continually do good, to be rich in good deeds, and to be generous and willing to share, so that I will lay up treasure for myself as a firm foundation for the coming age, and so that I may take hold of the life that is truly life!
(1 Timothy 6:17-19 NIV)

You say in Your Word, Lord, that trying to get rich quick is evil and leads to poverty, so make me a wise and generous person who trusts in You for Your provision. (Proverbs 28:22 TLB)

I pray that You would guard me from the love of money which causes me to never be satisfied with my income or my possessions. (Ecclesiastes 5:10 NIV)

Help me to remember that it is better to have little – with fear for the Lord – than to have great treasure and inner turmoil. (Proverbs 15:16 NLT)

Lord, I pray that instead of shame and dishonor, I will inherit a double portion of prosperity and joy! (Isaiah 61:7 NLT)

"Save now, we beseech You, O Lord; send now prosperity, O Lord, we beseech You, and give to us success!" (Psalm 118:25 AMP)

"Those who trust in the Lord shall be given every blessing." (Psalm 37:9 TLB)

"Those who seek the Lord shall not lack any good thing." (Psalm 34:10 NKJV)

"Fear the Lord, you His godly people, for those who fear Him will have all they need." (Psalm 34:9 NLT)

"For the Lord God is a sun and shield; the Lord gives grace and glory; no good thing does He withhold from those who walk uprightly. O Lord of hosts, How blessed is the man who trusts in You!" (Psalm 84:11-12 NASB)

Salvation

Dear God, I claim Your promise which says that because I believe in the Lord Jesus, I will be saved – along with my entire household. (Acts 16:31 NLT)

I thank You, Lord, that You will deliver those for whom I intercede who are not innocent, for they will be delivered through the cleanness of my hands. (Job 22:30 AMP)

Lord, I ask that You give [my loved ones] eyes to see, ears to hear, and hearts to understand, so that they would turn to You, and You would heal them. (John 12:40 NLT)

Open their eyes, Lord; turn them from darkness to light, from the power of Satan to You, God, so that they may receive forgiveness of sins, and a place among those who are sanctified by faith in Jesus Christ, in whose holy name I pray. (Acts 26:17-18 NIV)

Grant them repentance, Lord. Lead them to a knowledge of the truth. Grant that they may come to their senses and escape the devil's snares and make Jesus the Lord of their lives. Grant that they may prove their repentance by their deeds. (2 Timothy 2:25-26 NIV)

Lord, send forth Your Holy Spirit to open their minds and hearts to receive the truth, and to act on it. (John 14:16-17 NIV)

I pray that those who are in error will believe the truth, and that complainers and criticizers will be willing to be taught in Jesus' name. (Isaiah 29:24 TLB)

Dear Lord, cure them of idolatry, faithlessness, and backsliding, and let Your love for them know no bounds! (Hosea 14:4 TLB)

You have seen what they do, Lord, but You will heal them anyway! You will lead them and comfort them, helping them to mourn and to confess their sins. (Isaiah 57:18 TLB)

O God, help me to live a godly life that will speak to them better than any words. (1 Peter 3:2 TLB)

Lord, You say in Your Word that You want all people to be saved and to come to a knowledge of the truth, so please save my loved ones! (1 Timothy 2:3-4)

O God, who said "Let there be light in the darkness," I ask that You make Your light shine in the hearts of my loved ones so they may know the glory of God that is seen in the face of Jesus Christ! (2 Corinthians 4:6 NLT)

Witnessing/Ministry

Thank You, Lord, for giving me Your Holy Spirit to fill me with power, ability, efficiency, and might – so that I can testify about You with great effect! (Acts 1:8 AMP/TLB)

I am sent by God, and I speak the words of God, for the Spirit of God is upon me without measure or limit. (John 3:34 NLT)

I will not worry about what to say, or how to say it, for My Father's Spirit will give me the right words at the right time. (Matthew 10:19-20 NIV/NLT)

Lord, I pray that whatever I say is just what You want me to say. (John 12:50 NIV)

I pray that my teaching is not my own, but it comes from You who sent me. (John 7:16 NIV)

Dear God, help me to keep a close watch on all I do and think. Help me to stay true to what is right, so that You can BLESS me and USE me to help others. (1 Timothy 4:16 TLB)

I thank You, Lord, that You have given me strength to do Your work, and You have considered me faithful, appointing me to Your service. (1 Timothy 1:12 NIV)

Lord, I pray that I may finish my course with joy, and the ministry which I have obtained from You, and which

You have entrusted to me, and that I will faithfully attest to the Gospel of God's grace – Your unmerited favor, spiritual blessings, and mercy! (Acts 20:24 AMP)

Help me to always remain calm, cool, and steady, Lord – accepting and suffering unflinchingly every hardship, doing the work of an evangelist, and fully performing all the duties of my ministry. (2 Timothy 4:5 AMP)

Lord, help me to faithfully care for the flock that You have entrusted to me. Teach me how to watch over them willingly, and not grudgingly – not for what I will get out of it, but because I am eager to serve You. Please work in my heart so that I will never be tempted to lord it over the people You have assigned to my care. Instead, help me to lead them by my own good example. Remind me often that Your Word says that those of us who teach will be judged by a higher standard than others, and that we assume the greater accountability. Thank You that when the Great Shepherd appears, I will receive a crown of never-ending glory and honor! (1 Peter 5:2-4 NLT; James 3:1 AMP)

Dear Lord, I ask You to help me to preach the Word of God urgently at all times, whenever I get the chance, in season and out, when it is convenient, and when it is not – correcting, warning, and rebuking my people when they need it, encouraging them to do right, all the time feeding them patiently with Your Word. Help me to stand firm in my faith, unfazed by those who don't want to listen to the Truth, but will go around looking for teachers who will tell them just what they want to hear. I choose not to be afraid of suffering for You, Lord, but to stay focused on bringing others to Christ, leaving nothing undone that I ought to do, fully performing all the duties of my ministry. (2 Timothy 4:2-5 TLB)

Lord, I ask that You use me in greater ways to equip Your people to do Your work, and to build up the Church, the Body of Christ. (Ephesians 4:12 NLT)

Dear God, help me to devote myself to Your Word, for You have said: "All Scripture is inspired by God and is useful to teach us what is true, and to make us realize what is wrong in our lives. It corrects us when we are wrong and teaches us to do what is right. God uses it to prepare and equip His people to do every good work." Hallelujah! (2 Timothy 3:16-17 NLT)

Strength

"I will go in the strength of the Lord God." (Psalm 71:16 NKJV)

"New honors are constantly bestowed on me, and my strength is continually renewed." (Job 29:20 NLT)

Lord, help me to seek and deeply long for You and Your strength, Your power, and Your might at all times. Teach me to deeply long for Your face and Your presence continually! (Psalm 105:4 AMP)

O Lord, be gracious to me – I long for You! Be my strength every morning, my salvation in time of distress. (Isaiah 33:2 NIV)

Fill me with strength, O Lord, and protect me wherever I go. (Psalm 32 TLB)

It is written, "Let the weak say, 'I am strong – a warrior!'" (Joel 3:10 AMP)

"When I pray, You answer me; You encourage me by giving me the strength I need." (Psalm 138:3 NLT)

Make me strong in You, Lord – empowered through my union with You. Teach me how to draw my strength from You – that strength which Your boundless might provides. (Ephesians 6:10 AMP)

"I am honored in the sight of the Lord, and My God is My strength." (Isaiah 49:5 NASB)

"What a wonderful God we have – He is the Father of our Lord Jesus Christ, the source of every mercy, and the One who wonderfully comforts and strengthens us in our hardships and trials." (2 Corinthians 1:3 TLB)

Lord, help me to have the kind of relationship with You that will make me supernaturally strong, and enable me to carry out great exploits. (Daniel 11:32 NKJV)

"He gives power to those who are tired and worn out; He offers strength to the weak. But those who wait on the Lord will find new strength. They will fly high on wings like eagles. They will run and not grow weary. They will walk and not faint." (Isaiah 40:29,31 NLT)

Heavenly Father, God of my Master Jesus Christ, the God of glory, I ask that you make me intelligent and discerning in knowing You personally, my eyes focused and clear, so that I can see exactly what it is You are calling me to do, and grasp the immensity of this glorious way of life that You have for Your followers, the utter extravagance of Your work in those of us who trust in You – *endless energy and boundless strength!* (Ephesians 1:18 MSG)

I pray that from Your glorious, unlimited resources, You will give me mighty inner strength through Your Holy Spirit. (Ephesians 3:16 NLT)

Dear God, help me to keep my spiritual eyes open so that I can watch out for attacks from the devil, who prowls around like a roaring lion, looking for some victim to devour. Help me to take a firm stand against him, and to be strong in my faith at all times. (1 Peter 5:8-9 NLT)

O Lord, I pray that my determined purpose would be to know You more deeply and intimately, perceiving and recognizing and understanding the wonders of You more strongly and more clearly – and that I may in that same way come to know the mighty power outflowing from Your resurrection! (Philippians 3:10 AMP)

O Lord my God, fill me with Your mighty, glorious strength so that I can keep going no matter what happens – always full of the joy of the Lord, and always thankful to You for making me fit to share in all the wonderful things that belong to those of us who live in the Kingdom of Light. (Colossians 1:11-12 TLB)

"I was pushed back and about to fall, but the Lord helped me. The Lord is my strength and my defense; He has become my salvation." (Psalm 118:13-14 NIV)

Lord, grant me a cheerful heart that is good medicine to my body, and protect me from a broken spirit which can sap my strength. (Proverbs 17:22 NLT)

Turn to me and have mercy on me, Lord. Grant me your strength and save me! (Psalm 86:16 NIV)

"O Lord God, please remember me and please strengthen me." (Judges 16:28 NASB)

Lord, make me strong and courageous to set about the work You assign to me. Don't let me be frightened by the size of the task, but remind me that You will be with me all the way, and You will not forsake me. You will see to it that everything is finished correctly.
(1 Chronicles 28:20 TLB)

Dear God, I ask You to give me a wise mind, and a spirit attuned to Your will, so that I can have a thorough understanding of the ways in which You work. I pray that I would live well for the Master, making You proud of me, as I work hard for Your kingdom. May I learn more and more how YOU work, so that I may learn better and better how to do MY work. I pray that I will have the strength to stick it out over the long haul – not the grim strength of gritting my teeth, but the glory-strength that God gives. Thank You for giving me the strength that endures the unendurable, and spills over into joy, thanking the Father who empowers me to take part in everything bright and beautiful that He has for me! (Colossians 1:9-12 MSG)

"The Lord is my strength, my shield from every danger. I trust in Him with all my heart. He helps me, and my heart is filled with joy. I burst out in songs of thanksgiving." (Psalm 28:7 NLT)

"You are my strength; I wait for You to rescue me, for You, O God, are my fortress. In His unfailing love, my God will stand with me. He will let me look down in triumph on all my enemies." (Psalm 59:9-10 NLT)

O Lord, fill me with unyielding and impenetrable strength, and bless me with Your peace. (Psalm 29:11 AMP)

I say to myself – "Do not grieve or be depressed, for the joy of the Lord is your strength and stronghold!" (Nehemiah 8:10 AMP)

Greater is He who is in me, than he who is in the world! (1 John 4:4 NASB)

O Lord, help me to be strong with the strength Christ Jesus gives me. (2 Timothy 2:1 TLB)

My Father is greater than all, and His Spirit lives in me! (John 10:29 NIV)

O God of peace, make me entirely pure and devoted to You. Keep my spirit, soul, and body strong and blameless until that day when our Lord Jesus Christ comes back again. Thank You that You have called me to become Your child, and You will do all this for me, just as You promised! (1 Thessalonians 5:23 TLB)

Lord, give me a strong spirit that will sustain me in bodily pain or trouble, and guard me from a weak or broken spirit. (Proverbs 18:14 AMP)

O Lord, strengthen me and protect me from the evil one. (2 Thessalonians 3:3 NIV)

Give me new strength, Lord. Help me to do what honors You the most. (Psalm 23:3 TLB)

I say to myself – "Be strong and do not give up, for your work will be rewarded!" (2 Chronicles 15:7 NIV)

O God, increase me greatly, and make me stronger than my enemies. (Psalm 105:24 NKJV)

"Never forget Your promises to me Your servant, for they are my only hope. They give me strength in all my troubles; how they refresh and revive me!" (Psalm 119:49-50 TLB)

O God of grace – who imparts all blessing and favor – I ask that You make me what I ought to be, establish and ground me securely, and strengthen and settle me!
(1 Peter 5:10 AMP)

"God is our refuge and strength, always ready to help in times of trouble." (Psalm 46:1 NLT)

I pray that just as I accepted Christ Jesus as my Lord, I will continue to live in obedience to Him. May my roots grow down into Him and draw up nourishment from Him, so that I will grow in faith, strong and vigorous in the truth I was taught. May my life overflow with thanksgiving for all He has done. And I pray that I will never let anyone lead me astray with empty philosophies and high-sounding nonsense that come from human thinking and from the evil powers of this world, instead of from Christ. (Colossians 2:6-8 NLT)

Help me to keep my eyes open for spiritual danger, Lord. Empower me to stay true to You at all times. Make me courageous and strong. (1 Corinthians 16:13 TLB)

"The Lord God is my strength, my personal bravery and my invincible army; He makes my feet like hinds' feet, and will make me to walk [not to stand still in terror, but to walk] and make [spiritual] progress upon my high places [of trouble, suffering or responsibility]!" (Habakkuk 3:19 AMP)

"The salvation of the righteous is from the LORD; He is their strength in time of trouble. The Lord helps them and delivers them; He delivers them from the wicked and saves them, because they take refuge in Him." (Psalm 37:39-40 NASB)

Our Words

Lord, I do want to live a long, prosperous life, and to see many good days – so help me to keep my tongue from speaking evil, and my lips from telling lies. (Psalm 34:12-13 NIV/NLT)

Lord, teach me to watch what I do, and to not sin in what I say. I am determined to hold my tongue, especially when the ungodly are around me. I have resolved that my mouth will not sin against You or others. (Psalm 39:1 NLT; Psalm 17:3 NIV)

Help me to always speak the truth in love, growing in every way more and more like Christ! (Ephesians 4:15 NLT)

"Set a guard, O LORD, over my mouth; keep watch over the door of my lips." (Psalm 141:3 NASB)

May my spoken words and unspoken thoughts be pleasing to You, O Lord my Rock and my Redeemer! (Psalm 19:14 TLB)

I pray, Lord, that the reply of my tongue will always come from You, and that YOU will always have the last Word. (Proverbs 16:1 NIV/MSG)

May my mouth continually overflow with words that help and heal, and may I refuse to speak cutting words that wound and maim. (Proverbs 15:4 MSG)

Lord, help me to guard my lips so that my life will be protected and preserved, according to Your Word. Don't let me speak rashly, so that I bring ruin or calamity upon myself. I choose to watch my tongue and to keep my mouth shut, so that I will stay out of trouble! (Proverbs 13:3 NIV; Proverbs 21:23 NIV)

On the basis of Your Word, help me to put away from me all false and dishonest speech, and to put far from me all willful and contrary talk. I pray that I would never talk out of both sides of my mouth, and that I would avoid all careless banter, white lies, and gossip. (Proverbs 4:24 AMP/MSG)

Lord, when I speak, let me always have something worthwhile to say, and to say it kindly. (Proverbs 31:26 MSG)

Remind me often, dear Lord, that death and life are in the power of the tongue, and that I will bear the consequences of my words. (Proverbs 18:21 AMP)

Help me to hold my tongue when it's the smartest thing for me to do, Lord, and remind me that it's to my credit to restrain my anger and overlook an insult. (Proverbs MSG/TLB)

Dear God, help me to watch the way I talk. I pray that I would let nothing foul or dirty come out of my mouth, and that I would say only what is helpful, each word a gift. May I never grieve You, or break Your heart.

Remind me often that Your Holy Spirit, moving and breathing within me, is the most intimate part of my life, making me fit for You. Help me to never take such a precious gift for granted. Enable and empower me to make a clean break with all backbiting, cutting remarks, and profane talk. Make me gentle and sensitive toward others, always forgiving them as quickly and thoroughly as God in Christ forgave me. (Ephesians 4:29-32 MSG)

Help me to steer clear of foolish discussions which lead people into the sin of anger with each other, since things could be said that will burn and hurt for a long time to come. (2 Timothy 2:16-17 TLB)

Help me to keep in mind that, in the end, people appreciate honest criticism far more than flattery. (Proverbs 28:23 NLT)

Lord, make me shrewd and wise as a serpent, and innocent and guileless as a dove. Give me words and wisdom which none of my adversaries can resist, deny, take exception to, or contradict. Thank You that by Your grace, I will not worry about what to say, or how to say it – for Your Spirit will give me the right words at the right time! (Matthew 10:16 NASB; Luke 21:15 NKJV; Matthew 10:19-20 NLT)

Make me a trustworthy person who can keep a secret, instead of being a gossip who betrays a confidence. (Proverbs 11:13 NLT)

O Sovereign Lord, give me Your words of wisdom, so that I may know how to comfort the weary, and open my understanding to Your will each morning. (Isaiah 50:4 NLT)

O Lord, guard my tongue from reckless words that pierce and cut, and fill my mouth with words that soothe and heal. (Proverbs 12:18 TLB)

Make me a truly wise person who uses few words, Lord, and give me the understanding that makes me cool and even-tempered – for Your Word says that even fools are thought to be wise when they keep silent, and when they keep their mouths shut, they seem intelligent! (Proverbs 17:27-28 NLT)

I pray that I would always offer others good counsel, and that I would teach them right from wrong. May I make Your law my own, Lord, so that I will never slip from Your path. (Psalm 34:30-31 NLT)

O God, help me to watch my words and hold my tongue, so that I will save myself a lot of grief! (Proverbs 21:23 MSG)

Help me to remember, Lord, that patient persistence pierces through indifference, and gentle speech breaks down rigid defenses. (Proverbs 25:15 MSG)

Remind me often, Lord, that a word out of my mouth may seem of no account, but it can accomplish nearly anything – or destroy it! Just as it only takes a spark to set off a forest fire, a careless or wrongly placed word out of my mouth can do that. (James 3:5 MSG)

Since gossips can't keep secrets, please help me to never confide in blabbermouths, Lord. (Proverbs 20:19 MSG)

"Fire goes out for lack of fuel, and tensions disappear when gossip stops. A quarrelsome man starts fights as easily as a match sets fire to paper." (Proverbs 26:20-21)

Love

Lord, I pray that my love for others would always be sincere – the real thing without guile or hypocrisy. Help me to hate what is evil, to detest all ungodliness, and to never tolerate wickedness. Teach me how to hold on tightly to what is good, and to always stand on the side of good. (Romans 12:9 AMP/TLB)

Dear God, help me to imitate You in everything I do, because I am Your dearly loved child. Enable me to live a life filled with love, following the example of Christ, who loved us and offered Himself as a sacrifice for us, a pleasing aroma to God. (Ephesians 5:1-2 NLT)

I pray that I would get rid of all bitterness, rage, anger, harsh words, slander, and all types of evil behavior. I pray that instead, I would always be kind and compassionate toward others, forgiving them just as God through Christ forgave me. (Ephesians 4:31-32 NLT)

Above all, I pray that I would have fervent and unfailing love for others, because love covers a multitude of sins – it overlooks unkindness, and unselfishly seeks the best for others. (1 Peter 4:8 AMP)

Lord, help me to keep Your command which tells me to love and unselfishly seek the best for others, especially for my fellow believers. (John 15:17 AMP)

Remind me, Lord, that love prospers when a fault is forgiven, but dwelling on it separates even the closest of friends. (Proverbs 17:9 NLT)

Teach me how to live by the principles of love and justice, and to always be expecting much from You, my God. (Hosea 12:6 TLB)

Lord, help me to love myself and everyone else with Your kind of love. Make me patient and kind. Guard me from jealousy, envy, pride, and boasting. Help me to resist being rude or irritable, cranky or touchy. Enable me to refuse to keep a record of wrongs, or to demand my own way. Remind me that Your kind of love never gives up, never loses faith, and is always hopeful, and endures through every circumstance.
(1 Corinthians 13:4-7 NLT)

I pray that, in everything, I will always treat people the same way that I want them to treat me. (Matthew 7:12 NASB)

Lord, help me to walk in forgiveness at all times so that Satan cannot outsmart me, for I am not unaware of his evil schemes. (2 Corinthians 2:10-11 NLT)

I thank You, Lord, that my hope in Your promises will never disappoint me, because You have abundantly poured out Your love within my heart through the Holy Spirit whom You have given me. (Romans 5:5 AMP)

Dear God, I pray that as Your chosen one, holy and dearly loved, I would clothe myself with tenderhearted mercy, kindness, humility, gentleness, and patience. Teach me to make allowance for others' faults, and to forgive anyone who offends me. Help me to remember that as You forgave me, I must forgive others. Above all, may I clothe myself with love, which binds us all together in perfect harmony. And may the peace that comes from Christ rule in my heart, for You have called me to live in peace. And grant me a heart that continually overflows with thanksgiving. (Colossians 3:12-15 NLT)

O Lord, cause my faith to grow more and more, and make the love I have for others continually increase. (2 Thessalonians 1:3 NIV)

Help me to stop just SAYING that I love people, and to REALLY love them, and to SHOW IT by my ACTIONS. (1 John 3:18 TLB)

Dear Lord, teach me how to love my enemies, and to pray for those who persecute me, as You have commanded. For then I will be acting as a true child of God – for You give sunlight to both the evil and the good, and You send rain on the just and the unjust, too. (Matthew 5:44-45 NLT)

Teach me how to pursue righteousness and love, so that I will find the life, prosperity, and honor that You promise in Your Word. (Proverbs 21:21 NIV)

Remind me, Lord, that You require me to act justly, to love mercy, and to walk humbly with my God at all times. (Micah 6:8 NIV)

On the basis of Your Word, I pray that I would never let mercy, kindness, and truth forsake me (shutting out all hatred, selfishness, hypocrisy, and falsehood). May I bind them around my neck and write them on the tablet of my heart – for then I shall find favor, good understanding, and high esteem in the sight of God and man. (Proverbs 3:3-4 AMP)

Lord, show me how to stir into flame the strength and boldness that is in me, for the Holy Spirit – Your gift to me – does not want me to be afraid of people, but to be wise and strong, and to love them and enjoy being with them. Help me to never be afraid to tell others about You, Lord. (2 Timothy 1:6-8 TLB)

Teach me to be an example to all believers in what I say, in the way I live, in my love, my faith, and my purity. (1 Timothy 4:12 NLT)

Let me experience the love of Christ, though it is too great to understand fully, so that I will be made complete with all the fullness of life and power that comes from God. (Ephesians 3:19 NLT)

O Lord my God, I beseech You to help me live a life that is worthy of the divine calling to which I have been called – that is, to live a life that exhibits godly character, moral courage, personal integrity, and mature behavior – a life that expresses gratitude to God for my salvation, with all humility (forsaking self-righteousness), and gentleness (maintaining self-control), with patience, bearing with others in unselfish love. (Ephesians 4:1-2 AMP)

Grief and Sorrow

Lord, on the basis of Your Word, I ask that You heal my broken heart, bind up my wounds, and cure my pains and sorrows. (Psalm 147:3 AMP)

I take Your Word, Lord, which says that You will not leave me as an orphan – comfortless, desolate, bereaved, forlorn, or helpless – but You will come to me and draw me close. (John 14:18 AMP)

You have promised to help the fallen, and to lift those bent beneath their loads, so raise me up now, Lord, and give me a fresh start. (Psalm 145:14 NLT/MSG)

Lord, Your Word says that You are especially close to those whose hearts are breaking. Please grant me Your discernible presence now, and help me to catch my breath. (Psalm 34:18 TLB/MSG)

You said, Lord, that I am blessed when I feel as though I have lost what is most dear to me, because only then can I be embraced by the One most dear to me. Let me feel Your embrace now in healing, comforting, and life-changing ways. (Matthew 5:4 MSG)

Even if my mother and my father abandon me, Lord, I thank You that You will welcome me, comfort me, and hold me close. You will take care of me, and You will meet all my needs. (Psalm 27:10 TLB/NKJV; Philippians 4:19 NIV)

Lord, I thank You that You will not ignore or belittle my suffering. You will not turn Your back on me or walk away. You are right here, listening and responding to my cries for help. (Psalm 22:24 NLT)

Lord, You said, "Blessed are those who mourn, for they will be comforted." I'm holding You to Your Word, Lord, and I'm asking You and trusting You to grant me Your supernatural comfort now for my spirit, soul, and body. (Matthew 5:4 NIV)

Deliver me from a spirit of heaviness and despair, and clothe me in a garment of praise and thanksgiving. Whenever sorrow or sadness threaten to overwhelm me, help me to lift my hands and declare, "Yet I will rejoice in the Lord! I will be joyful in God my Savior!" (Isaiah 61:3 NLT/TLB; Habakkuk 3:18 NIV)

Thank You, Lord, that you will yet fill my mouth with laughter and my lips with shouts of joy! (Job 8:20-21 NIV)

O Lord, comfort me as a loving mother comforts her beloved child. (Isaiah 66:13 NIV)

I claim Your promise, Lord, which says that I will surely forget my troubles, recalling them only as waters gone by. (Job 11:16 NIV)

"Though you have made me see troubles, many and bitter, You will restore my life again; from the depths of the earth You will again bring me up. You will increase my honor and comfort me once more." (Psalm 71:20-21 NIV)

"But, O my soul, don't be discouraged. Don't be upset. Expect God to act! For I know that I shall again have plenty of reason to praise Him for all that He will do. He is my help! He is my God!" (Isaiah 42:11 TLB)

"You, O Lord, keep my lamp burning; my God turns my darkness into light." (Psalm 18:28 NIV)

"I am still confident of this: I will see the goodness of the Lord in the land of the living. Wait for the Lord; be strong and take heart and wait for the Lord!" (Psalm 27:13-14 NIV)

"I have told you these things, so that in Me you may have [perfect] peace and confidence. In the world you have tribulation and trials and distress and frustration; but be of good cheer [take courage; be confident, certain, undaunted]! For I have overcome the world. [I have deprived it of power to harm you and have conquered it for you.]" (John 16:33 AMP)

"Those who sow with tears will reap with songs of joy. Those who go out weeping, carrying seed to sow, will return with songs of joy, carrying sheaves with them." (Psalm 126:5-6 NIV)

"Arise [from the depression and prostration in which circumstances have kept you – rise to a new life]! Shine (be radiant with the glory of the Lord), for your light has come, and the glory of the Lord has risen upon you!" (Isaiah 60:1 AMP)

Anger

Dear Lord, when others bad-mouth or belittle me – when they insult me or cause me to suffer somehow – help me to follow Christ's example by refusing to retaliate, and by leaving my case in Your hands, for You always judge fairly. (1 Peter 2:23 NLT)

Lord, I pray that I would never allow anger to control me, but that I would always get over my anger quickly – and always before the sun goes down – so that I won't give a foothold to the devil. (Ephesians 4:26-27 NLT)

Help me to steer clear of foolish discussions which lead people into the sin of anger with each other, since things could be said that will burn and hurt for a long time to come. (2 Timothy 2:16-17 TLB)

Remind me, Lord, that avoiding a fight is a mark of honor, and that only fools insist on quarreling. (Proverbs 20:3 NLT)

When someone insults me, help me to remain cool and calm, instead of losing my temper. (Proverbs 12:16 NLT)

Don't let me stir up strife by being hot-tempered. Instead, make me slow to anger and patient at all times, so that I can calm disputes and keep the peace. (Proverbs 15:18 AMP)

I pray that I would get rid of all bitterness, rage, anger, harsh words, slander, and all types of evil behavior. I pray that instead, I would always be kind and compassionate toward others, forgiving them just as quickly and thoroughly as God through Christ forgave me. (Ephesians 4:31-32 NLT)

O Lord, make me quick to hear (a ready listener), slow to speak, and slow to take offense and to get angry. For man's anger does not promote the righteousness that You wish and require. (James 1:19-20 AMP)

Guard me from a quick temper which can cause me to do foolish things that I will regret later on. (Proverbs 14:17 NIV/MSG)

Lord, Your Word says that anger boomerangs, and that a fool can be spotted by the lumps on his head, so please don't let me be quick to fly off the handle! (Ecclesiastes 7:9 MSG)

I don't want to be an angry person who starts fights and commits all kinds of sin, so please help me to control my temper. (Proverbs 29:22 NLT)

Teach me how to give a gentle answer that turns away wrath, and to avoid harsh words that cause quarrels. (Proverbs 15:1 TLB)

O God, I pray that I would rid myself of anger, rage, malicious behavior, slander, hatred, cursing, lying, and dirty language. I pray that I would strip off my old sinful nature and all its wicked deeds, and that I would put on my new nature, and be renewed as I learn to know You better, and become more like You. (Colossians 3:8-10 NLT)

"If your enemy is hungry, give him food! If he is thirsty, give him something to drink! This will make him feel ashamed of himself, and God will reward you." (Proverbs 25:21-22 TLB)

"Dear friends, never avenge yourselves. Leave that to God, for He has said that He will repay those who deserve it. Don't take the law into your own hands. Instead, feed your enemy if he is hungry. If he is thirsty give him something to drink and you will be 'heaping coals of fire on his head.' In other words, he will feel ashamed of himself for what he has done to you. Don't let evil get the upper hand, but conquer evil by doing good." (Romans 12:19-21 TLB)

"But I say, if you are even angry with someone, you are subject to judgment! If you call someone an idiot, you are in danger of being brought before the court. And if you curse someone, you are in danger of the fires of hell." (Matthew 5:22 NLT)

Overcoming Bad Habits

I walk by the Spirit, and I will NOT carry out the desires of the flesh. (Galatians 5:16 NASB)

I think clearly and I exercise self-control. I look forward to the special blessings that will come to me at the return of Jesus Christ! (1 Peter 1:13 NLT)

I belong to Jesus Christ, and I have crucified the flesh with its passions, appetites, and desires. I live by the Spirit, and I keep in step with the Spirit. (Galatians 24-25 NIV)

By the Spirit, I put to death the misdeeds of my body that I may live. For I am led by the Spirit of God and I am a child of God! (Romans 8:13-14 NIV)

I discipline my body and make it my slave. I exercise self-control in all things. (1 Corinthians 9:27 NASB; 1 Corinthians 9:25 NASB)

I clothe myself with the Lord Jesus Christ, and I make no provision for the flesh, to fulfill its lusts. (Romans 13:14 NKJV)

I train myself to be godly. For physical training is of some value, but godliness has value for all things, holding promise for both the present life and the life to come. (1 Timothy 4:7-8 NIV)

I am always clear minded and self-controlled so that I can pray. (1 Peter 4:7 NIV)

"I have been crucified with Christ and I no longer live, but Christ lives in me. The life I now live in the body, I live by faith in the Son of God, who loved me and gave Himself for me." (Galatians 2:20 NIV)

I am self-controlled and alert, because my enemy the devil prowls around like a roaring lion looking for someone to devour. I resist him, standing firm in my faith, because I know that my brothers and sisters in Christ throughout the world are undergoing the same kind of sufferings. (1 Peter 5:8-9 NIV)

As I come to know Jesus better and better, His divine power gives me everything I need for living a godly life. He has called me to receive His own glory and goodness! (2 Peter 1:3 NLT)

I am sensible and self-controlled, and I always behave wisely, taking life seriously. In all things, I show myself to be an example of good works, having the strictest regard for integrity and truth, so that those who oppose my faith will be ashamed, having nothing bad to say about me. (Titus 2:6-8 AMP)

God has not given me a spirit of timidity or fear, but He has given me a spirit of power, love, discipline, and self-control. (2 Timothy 1:7 AMP)

The grace of God teaches me to say 'NO' to ungodliness and worldly passions, and to live a self-controlled, upright, and godly life in this present world. (Titus 2:11-12 NIV)

The Holy Spirit controls my life and produces in me love, joy, peace, patience, kindness, goodness, faithfulness, gentleness, and self-control. (Galatians 5:22 TLB)

I refuse to lack self-control and be like a city whose walls are broken down. (Proverbs 25:28 NIV)

Fear

Jesus has given me His own peace, so I refuse to let my heart be troubled or afraid. I will NOT allow myself to be agitated or disturbed. And I will NOT permit myself to be fearful, intimidated, cowardly, or unsettled. (John 14:27 AMP)

I will NOT be seized with alarm and struck with fear – I WILL KEEP ON BELIEVING! (Mark 5:36 AMP)

I have no fear of bad news. My heart is steadfast, trusting in the Lord. My heart is secure, I will have no fear; in the end, I will look in triumph on my enemies! (Psalm 112:7-8 NIV)

The Lord my God is with me. He is mighty to save. He will take great delight in me. He will calm all my fears with His love. He will give me victory. He will rejoice over me with singing! Hallelujah! (Zephaniah 3:17 NIV/NLT)

The Lord has cleared away my enemies; He Himself is in my midst. Never again will I fear any harm; I shall not see evil anymore! (Zephaniah 3:15 NASB/NIV)

God has NOT given me a spirit of fear or timidity, but a spirit of power, love, a sound mind, and self-control. Therefore, I shall never be ashamed or afraid to tell others about Christ! (2 Timothy 1:7-8 NLT/AMP)

"I sought the Lord, and He answered me; He delivered me from ALL my fears." (Psalm 34:4 NIV)

When I am tempted to be afraid, I will put my confidence in the Lord. Yes, I will trust the promises of God! And since I am trusting Him, what can mere man do to me? (Psalm 56:3-4 TLB)

I say with confidence, "The Lord is my Helper – I will NOT be afraid!" (Hebrews 13:6 NIV)

The Lord is my light and my salvation; whom shall I fear? The Lord is the strength of my life; of whom shall I be afraid? When the wicked come against me, they will stumble and fall! Yes, though a mighty army marches against me, my heart shall know no fear! I am confident that God will save me. (Psalm 27:1-3 NKJV/TLB)

With God on my side, I am fearless – afraid of no one and nothing! (Psalm 27:1 MSG)

The Lord pays attention to every area of my life, right down to the last detail. He has even numbered the hairs on my head! So I refuse to live in fear, or to be intimidated by people or circumstances. (Luke 12:6-7 MSG)

I refuse to think like everyone else does. I will not be afraid that some plan conceived behind closed doors will be the end of me. I will not fear anything except the Lord Almighty. He alone is the Holy One. Because I fear Him, I need fear nothing else. He will keep me safe! (Isaiah 8:11-14 NLT)

I will not be afraid, for I have been redeemed by the Lord. He has called me by name, and I belong to Him. When I go through deep waters, He will be with me. When I go through rivers of difficulty, I will not drown. When I walk through the fire of oppression, I will not be burned – the flames will not consume me. For I am precious to the Lord, I am honored in His sight, and He loves me! (Isaiah 43:1-2,4 NLT)

I will not be afraid, because those who are with US are more than those who are with THEM. (2 Kings 6:16 NIV)

I did not receive a spirit that makes me a slave to fear, but I received the Spirit of adoption, and by Him I cry, "Abba, Father!" (Romans 8:15 NIV)

"In my distress I prayed to the Lord, and He answered me and rescued me. He is for me! How can I be afraid? What can mere man do to me?" (Psalm 118:5-6 TLB)

I will study God's Word continually. I will meditate on it day and night so that I will be sure to obey everything written in it. Then I will prosper and succeed in all I do. I am strong and courageous. I will not be afraid or discouraged. For the Lord my God is with me wherever I go. (Joshua 1:8-9 NLT)

I will not be afraid of those who threaten me, for the time is coming when the truth will be revealed, and their secret plots will become public information. (Matthew 10:26 TLB)

"The very day I call for help, the tide of battle turns. My enemies flee! This one thing I know: GOD IS FOR ME! I am trusting God – oh, praise His promises! I am not afraid of anything mere man can do to me! Yes, praise His promises." (Psalm 56:9-11 TLB)

I am strong and courageous. I will not be afraid, and I WILL NOT PANIC. For the Lord my God will personally go ahead of me. He will neither fail me nor abandon me. (Deuteronomy 31:6 NLT)

The Lord shields and shelters me with His wings. His faithful promises are my armor. Now I don't need to be afraid of the dark anymore, nor fear the dangers of the day, nor the plagues of darkness, nor disasters in the morning. (Psalm 91:4-6 TLB)

I am firmly established in righteousness. I am far from even the thought of oppression, for I will not fear – and from terror, for it will not come near me. (Isaiah 54:14 AMP)

I will not be afraid, for I will not suffer shame. I will not fear disgrace, and I will not be humiliated. (Isaiah 54:4 NIV)

The Lord my God is holding me by my right hand, and He says to me, "Don't be afraid – I am here to help you!" Hallelujah! (Isaiah 41:13 TLB)

Even when I walk through the darkest valley, I will not be afraid, for the Lord is close beside me, guarding and guiding me all the way. (Psalm 23:4 TLB)

I will not be afraid. I will stand still – firm, confident, and undismayed – and I will see the deliverance the Lord will bring me. The Lord will fight for me, and I shall hold my peace and remain at rest. (Exodus 14:13,14 AMP)

I shall not be afraid of sudden disaster, or the destruction that comes upon the wicked – for the Lord is my security, and He will keep my foot from being caught in a trap! (Proverbs 3:25-26 NLT)

"See, God has come to save me. I will trust in Him and not be afraid. The Lord God is my strength and my song; He has given me victory." (Isaiah 12:2 NLT)

I will not be afraid, for I am deeply loved by God. I say to myself, "Be at peace, take heart, and be strong!" (Daniel 10:19 NLT)

Fearing people is a dangerous trap, so I choose to lean on, trust in, and put my confidence in the Lord, so that I shall be safe and set on high. (Proverbs 29:25 NLT/AMP)

I will not be afraid, but I will keep on speaking – I will not be silent. For the Lord has promised to be with me, and no one is going to attack or harm me. (Acts 18:9-10 NIV)

I will not be afraid, for the Lord will protect me, and my reward will be great! (Genesis 15:1 NLT)

I refuse to be upset or afraid. I will trust God, and everything will be all right! (Luke 8:50 MSG)

When I lie down, I will not be afraid; when I lie down, my sleep will be sweet! (Proverbs 3:24 NIV)

I lie down and sleep. Then I'm up again – rested, tall, and steady, for the Lord watches over me. I am fearless before my enemies coming at me from all sides. (Psalm 3:5-6 NIV/MSG)

God has promised to rescue me, and to make me both a symbol and a source of blessing – so I refuse to be afraid or discouraged. (Zechariah 8:13 NLT)

Prayer

"You who [are His servants and by your prayers] put the Lord in remembrance [of His promises], keep not silence, and give Him no rest..." (Isaiah 62:6-7 AMP)

"I love the Lord because He hears and answers my prayers. Because He bends down and listens, I will pray as long as I have breath!" (Psalm 116:1-2 NLT)

"Again, I tell you that if two of you on earth agree about anything you ask for, it will be done for you by My Father in heaven. For where two or three come together in My name, there am I with them." (Matthew 18:19-20 NIV)

"And Jesus answered saying to them, 'Have faith in God. Truly I say to you, whoever says to this mountain, "Be taken up and cast into the sea," and does not doubt in his heart, but believes that what he says is going to happen, it will be granted him. Therefore I say to you, all things for which you pray and ask, believe that you have received them, and they will be granted you.'" (Mark 11:22-24 NASB)

"Whenever you stand praying, if you have anything against anyone, forgive him [drop the issue, let it go], so that your Father who is in heaven will also forgive you your transgressions and wrongdoings [against Him and others]." (Mark 11:25 AMP)

"One day Jesus told His disciples a story to illustrate their need for constant prayer, and to show them that they must keep praying until the answer comes." (Luke 18:1 TLB)

"Whatever you ask in My name, that will I do, so that the Father may be glorified in the Son. If you ask Me anything in My name, I will do it." (John 14:13-14 NASB)

"Ask and keep on asking and you will receive, so that your joy (gladness, delight) may be full and complete." (John 16:24 AMP)

"In the same way, the Spirit helps us in our weakness. We do not know what we ought to pray for, but the Spirit Himself intercedes for us with groans that words cannot express. And He who searches our hearts knows the mind of the Spirit, because the Spirit intercedes for the saints in accordance with God's will." (Romans 8:26-27 NIV)

"Now to Him Who, by (in consequence of) the [action of His] power that is at work within us, is able to [carry out His purpose and] do superabundantly, far over and above all that we [dare] ask or think [infinitely beyond our highest prayers, desires, thoughts, hopes, or dreams] – to Him be glory in the church and in Christ Jesus throughout all generations forever and ever. Amen (so be it)." (Ephesians 3:20-21 AMP)

"And the seeds that fell on the good soil represent honest, good-hearted people who hear God's word, cling to it, and patiently produce a huge harvest." (Luke 8:15 NLT)

"So if you sinful people know how to give good gifts to your children, how much more will your heavenly Father give good gifts to those who ask Him." (Matthew 7:11 NLT)

"What I want from you is your true thanks; I want your promises fulfilled. I want you to trust Me in your times of trouble, so I can rescue you and you can give Me glory." (Psalm 50:15 TLB)

"Is anyone among you suffering? He should keep on praying about it." (James 5:13 TLB)

"Therefore, confess your sins to one another, and pray for one another so that you may be healed. The effective prayer of a righteous man can accomplish much." (James 5:16 NASB)

"Never stop praying." (1 Thessalonians 5:17 NLT)

"When you pray, go into your room, and when you have shut your door, pray to your Father who is in the secret place; and your Father who sees in secret will reward you openly." (Matthew 6:6 NKJV)

"The end and culmination of all things is near. Therefore, be sound-minded and self-controlled for the purpose of prayer [staying balanced and focused on the things of God so that your communication will be clear, reasonable, specific and pleasing to Him.]" (1 Peter 4:7 AMP)

"For I know the plans I have for you," declares the Lord, "plans to prosper you and not to harm you, plans to give you hope and a future. Then you will call upon Me and come and pray to Me, and I will listen to you. You will seek Me and find Me when you seek Me with all your heart." (Jeremiah 29:11-13 NIV)

"He will listen to the prayers of the destitute, for He is never too busy to heed their requests." (Psalm 102:17 TLB)

"When I pray, You answer me; You encourage me by giving me the strength I need." (Psalm 138:3 NLT)

"Do not be anxious about anything, but in every situation, by prayer and petition, with thanksgiving, present your requests to God. And the peace of God, which transcends all understanding, will guard your hearts and your minds in Christ Jesus." (Philippians 4:6-7 NIV)

"Rejoice always and delight in your faith; be unceasing and persistent in prayer; in every situation [no matter what the circumstances] be thankful and continually give thanks to God; for this is the will of God for you in Christ Jesus." (1 Thessalonians 5:16-18 AMP)

"Pray all the time. Ask God for anything in line with the Holy Spirit's wishes. Plead with Him, reminding Him of your needs, and keep praying earnestly for all Christians everywhere." (Ephesians 6:18 TLB)

"This is the confidence we have in approaching God: that if we ask anything according to His will, He hears us. And if we know that He hears us – whatever we ask – we know that we have what we asked of Him." (1 John 5:14-15 NIV)

"And we will receive from Him whatever we ask because we obey Him and do the things that please Him." (1 John 3:22 NLT)

"The Lord has heard my weeping. The Lord has heard my cry for mercy; the Lord accepts my prayer." (Psalm 6:8-9 NIV)

"I took my troubles to the LORD; I cried out to Him, and He answered my prayer." (Psalm 120:1 NLT)

"Draw near to God and He will draw near to you." (James 4:8 NKJV)

"Keep watching and praying, that you may not enter into temptation; the spirit it willing, but the flesh is weak." (Matthew 26:41 NASB)

"If we claim to be without sin, we deceive ourselves and the truth is not in us. If we confess our sins, He is faithful and just and will forgive us our sins and purify us from all unrighteousness. If we claim we have not sinned, we make Him out to be a liar and His word is not in us." (1 John 1:8-10 NIV)

"Don't burn out; keep yourselves fueled and aflame. Be alert servants of the Master, cheerfully expectant. Don't quit in hard times; pray all the harder." (Romans 12:12 MSG)

"I will answer them before they even call to Me. While they are still talking about their needs, I will go ahead and answer their prayers!" (Isaiah 65:24 NLT)

"You faithfully answer our prayers with awesome deeds, O God our Savior." (Psalm 65:5 NLT)

"And whatever you ask for in prayer, having faith and [really] believing, you will receive." (Matthew 21:22 AMP)

"If you remain in Me and My words remain in you [that is, if we are vitally united and My message lives in your heart], ask whatever you wish and it will be done for you." (John 15:7 AMP)

"For the eyes of the Lord are [looking favorably] upon the righteous (the upright), and His ears are attentive to their prayer (eager to answer)." (1 Peter 3:12 AMP)

"Keep on asking, and you will receive what you ask for. Keep on seeking, and you will find. Keep on knocking, and the door will be opened to you. For everyone who asks, receives. Everyone who seeks, finds. And to everyone who knocks, the door will be opened." (Matthew 7:7-8 NLT)

"Devote yourselves to prayer, keeping alert in it with an attitude of thanksgiving." (Colossians 4:2 NASB)

"I urge, then, first of all, that petitions, prayers, intercession and thanksgiving be made for all people – for kings and all those in authority, that we may live peaceful and quiet lives in all godliness and holiness." (1 Timothy 2:1-2 NIV)

"You have heard that it was said, 'Love your neighbor and hate your enemy.' But I tell you, love your enemies and pray for those who persecute you, that you may be children of your Father in heaven. He causes His sun to rise on the evil and the good, and sends rain on the righteous and the unrighteous." (Matthew 5:43-45)

"Prayer is essential in this ongoing warfare. Pray hard and long. Pray for your brothers and sisters. Keep your eyes open. Keep each other's spirits up so that no one falls behind or drops out." (Ephesians 6:18 MSG)

"Pray to the Lord day and night for the fulfillment of His promises. Take no rest, all you who pray. Give the Lord no rest..." (Isaiah 62:6 NLT)

"But the news about Him was spreading even farther, and large crowds were gathering to hear Him and to be healed of their sicknesses. But Jesus Himself would often slip away to the wilderness and pray." (Luke 5:15-16 NASB)

"He will even deliver the one [for whom you intercede] who is not innocent; yes, he will be delivered through the cleanness of your hands." (Job 22:30 AMP)

"And will not [our just] God defend and protect and avenge His elect (His chosen ones), who cry to Him day and night? Will He defer them and delay help on their behalf? I tell you, He will defend and protect and avenge them speedily. However, when the Son of Man comes, will He find [persistence in] faith on the earth?" (Luke 18:7-8 AMP)

"That's why I urge you to pray for absolutely everything, ranging from small to large. Include everything as you embrace this God-life, and you'll get God's everything." (Mark 11:24 MSG)

"Let us then approach the throne of grace with confidence, so that we may receive mercy and find grace to help us in our time of need." (Hebrews 4:16 NIV)

"In my distress I prayed to the Lord, and the Lord answered me and set me free. The Lord is for me, so I will have no fear. What can mere people do to me?" (Psalm 118:5-6 NLT)

"I am going to keep on being glad, for I know that as you pray for me, and as the Holy Spirit helps me, this is all going to turn out for my good." (Philippians 1:19 TLB)

"I will call upon the Lord to save me – and He will. I will pray morning, noon, and night, pleading aloud with God; and He will hear and answer." (Psalm 55:16-17 TLB)

"I'll deliver the surviving third to the refinery fires. I'll refine them as silver is refined, test them for purity as gold is tested. Then they'll pray to Me by name and I'll answer them personally. I'll say, 'That's My people.' They'll say, 'GOD – my God!'" (Zechariah 13:9 MSG)

"Lord, if You keep in mind our sins, then who can ever get an answer to his prayers? But You forgive! What an awesome thing this is! That is why I wait expectantly, trusting God to help, for He has promised." (Psalm 130:3-5 TLB)

"I thank You for answering my prayer and giving me victory!" (Psalm 118:21 NLT)

"I am the One who answers your prayers and cares for you." (Hosea 14:8 NLT)

"Let us test and examine our ways, and let us return to the Lord! Let us lift up our hearts and our hands [and then with them mount up in prayer] to God in heaven." (Lamentations 3:40-41 AMP)

"If I had not confessed the sin in my heart, the Lord would not have listened. But God did listen! He paid attention to my prayer." (Psalm 66:18-19 NLT)

"Because You answer prayer, all mankind will come to You with their requests." (Psalm 65:2 TLB)

"To You, O Lord, I pray. Don't fail me, Lord, for I am trusting You." (Psalm 25:1-2 TLB)

"They cried out to God in the battle, and He answered their prayers because they trusted in Him." (1 Chronicles 5:20 NASB)

"I have heard your prayer, I have seen your tears; surely I will heal you." (2 Kings 20:5 NKJV)

"In my desperation I prayed, and the Lord listened; He saved me from all my troubles." (Psalm 34:6 NLT)

"We will devote ourselves to prayer and to the ministry of the word." (Acts 6:4 NASB)

"Answer my prayers, O Lord, for Your unfailing love is wonderful. Take care of me, for Your mercy is so plentiful." (Psalm 69:16 NLT)

"If anyone turns a deaf ear to my instruction, even their prayers are detestable." (Proverbs 28:9 NIV)

"If I had cherished sin in my heart, the Lord would not have listened; but God has surely listened and heard my voice in prayer." (Psalm 66:18-19 NIV)

"Pour out your hearts like water to the Lord. Lift up your hands to Him in prayer, pleading for your children." (Lamentations 2:19 NLT)

Unity and Harmony

Dear God, I pray in the name of our Lord Jesus Christ, that all of us would be in perfect harmony and full agreement in what we say, and that there would be no dissensions or factions or divisions among us, but that we would be perfectly united in our common understanding and in our opinions and judgments, according to Your will. (1 Corinthians 1:10 AMP)

I pray that we would lead a life worthy of the calling we have received from You, Lord. May we always be humble and gentle, and patient with each other, making allowances for each other's faults because of our love. Help us to make every effort to keep ourselves united in the Spirit, binding ourselves together with peace. (Ephesians 4:1-3 NLT)

I pray that we would be devoted to one another with genuine affection, as members of one family, and that we would take delight in honoring each other, in obedience to You. (Romans 12:10 AMP/NLT)

Dear God who gives endurance and encouragement, give us the same attitude of mind toward each other that Christ Jesus had, so that with one mind and one voice, we may glorify and honor the God and Father of our Lord Jesus Christ. May we accept and welcome one another, just as Christ accepted us, in order to bring praise to our great God. (Romans 15:5-7 NIV/AMP)

I pray, Lord, that all of us would be like-minded, sympathetic, loving toward each other, and compassionate and humble. May we never repay evil with evil, or insult with insult. Instead, may we repay evil with blessing, because to this we were called so that we might inherit a blessing. (1 Peter 3:8-9 NIV)

Lord, let us find encouragement from belonging to Christ. Grant us comfort from His love, and fellowship together in the Spirit. Make our hearts tender and compassionate. May we always please You by loving one another, and agreeing wholeheartedly with each other, working together with one heart, one mind, and one purpose, according to Your will. (Philippians 2:1-2 NLT/TLB)

Promises for Parents

Dear Lord, help me to always see my children as a gift and a reward from You, and to continually give thanks for them. (Psalm 127:3 NLT)

Lord, I claim Your promise which says that because I believe in the Lord Jesus, I will be saved, along with everyone in my household! (Acts 16:31 NLT)

I claim Your promise, Lord, which says that all of my children shall be taught by You, and great shall be their peace and well-being. (Isaiah 54:13 NASB)

On the basis of Your Word, Lord, I ask that You deliver all of my descendants from all evil, harm, destruction, disease, and defeat! (Proverbs 11:21 NASB)

O Lord, contend with those who contend with me, and give safety to my children, and ease them day by day. (Isaiah 49:25 AMP)

O God, pour out Your Spirit upon my offspring, and Your blessing upon my descendants, according to Your Word. (Isaiah 44:3 NIV)

Thank You, Lord, that You will never forsake the righteous, and my children shall never have to beg for their bread. (Psalm 37:25 NIV)

O Lord, bless me richly, and cause me to continually increase – both me and my children. (Psalm 115:14 NLT/NIV)

As for me and my family, we will serve the Lord in Jesus' name! (Joshua 24:15 NLT)

O Lord, I thank You that You are on my side – defending my cause and rescuing my children! (Isaiah 49:25 MSG)

Help me to train up my children in the way they should go, and do not let them depart from it when they are older, Lord. (Proverbs 22:6 NKJV)

O God, cause my children to live in security, and to thrive in Your presence all their days. (Psalm 102:28 NLT)

Lord, I claim Your promise which says that Your Spirit, who is upon me, and Your words that You have put in my mouth will not depart from my mouth, or from the mouths of my children, or from the mouths of their descendants, from this time on and forever. Hallelujah! (Isaiah 59:21 NIV)

Help me to discipline my children while there is hope, so that I don't ruin their lives. (Proverbs 19:18 NLT)

Show me how to discipline my children, Lord, so that they give me peace of mind and make my heart glad. (Proverbs 29:17 NLT)

Help me to remember that a refusal to correct my children is a refusal to love them. Teach me to love my children by disciplining them according to Your will. (Proverbs 13:24 MSG)

O Lord, turn the hearts of my children to their parents, and the hearts of us parents to our children! (Malachi 4:6 NIV)

Lord, I pray that when my children get off-track, You will get them back on-track quickly – and when they complain and criticize, You will teach them gratitude and truth. (Isaiah 29:24 MSG)

O Lord my God, change my heart and the hearts of all my descendants, so that we will love You with all of our hearts and souls, and so we may live! (Deuteronomy 30:6 NLT)

I pray that I would obey You by teaching Your Word and Your commands to my children – by talking about them when we are at home and when we are on the road, when we are going to bed and when we are getting up. (Deuteronomy 11:19 NLT)

Dear God, please help me not to provoke or exasperate my children to the point of resentment with demands that are trivial, unreasonable, humiliating, or abusive. Guard me from showing favoritism or indifference to any of them. And teach me to bring them up tenderly, with lovingkindness, in the discipline and instruction of the Lord. (Ephesians 6:4 AMP)

I pray that I will never scold my children so much that they become discouraged and quit trying. (Colossians 3:21 TLB)

O God, I thank You that You have chosen me to direct my children, and my household after me, to keep the way of the Lord by doing what is right and just, so that You can do for me all that You have promised. (Genesis 18:19 NIV)

"Children are a gift from the Lord; they are a reward from Him." (Psalm 127:3 NLT)

"Grandchildren are the crowning glory of the aged; parents are the pride of their children." (Proverbs 17:6 NLT)

"You can be sure God will rescue the children of the godly." (Proverbs 11:21 TLB)

"Let each generation tell its children of Your mighty acts; let them proclaim Your power." (Psalm 145:4 NLT)

"Pour out your hearts like water to the Lord. Lift up your hands to Him in prayer, pleading for your children." (Lamentations 2:19 NLT)

"Therefore thus says the Lord, Who redeemed Abraham [out of Ur and idolatry], concerning the house of Jacob: Jacob shall not then be ashamed; not then shall his face become pale [with fear and disappointment because of his children's degeneracy]. For when he sees his children [walking in the way of piety and virtue], the work of My hands in his midst, they will revere My name; they will revere the Holy One of Jacob and reverently fear the God of Israel. Those who err in spirit will come to understanding, and those who murmur [discontentedly] will accept instruction." (Isaiah 29:22-24 AMP)

"This is what the Lord says: 'A voice is heard in Ramah, mourning and great weeping, Rachel weeping for her children and refusing to be comforted, because her children are no more.' This is what the Lord says: 'Restrain your voice from weeping and your eyes from tears, for your work will be rewarded,' declares the Lord. 'They will return from the land of the enemy. So there is hope for your future,' declares the Lord. 'Your children will return to their own land.'" (Jeremiah 31:15-17 NIV)

Childbearing

"He gives children to the childless wife, so that she becomes a happy mother. Hallelujah! Praise the Lord!" (Psalm 113:9 TLB)

"God gives childless couples a family, gives them joy as the parents of children. Hallelujah!" (Psalm 113:9 MSG)

"He will love you and bless you and give you many children." (Deuteronomy 7:13 NLT)

"You will be blessed more than any other people; none of your men or women will be childless."
(Deuteronomy 7:14 NIV)

"There will be no miscarriages or infertility among your people." (Exodus 23:26 NLT)

"Children are a gift from the Lord; they are a reward from Him." (Psalm 127:3 NLT)

"Worship the Lord your God, and His blessing will be on your food and water. I will take away sickness from among you, and none will miscarry or be barren in your land. I will give you a full life span." (Exodus 23:25-26 NIV)

"The Lord will give you prosperity in the land he swore to your ancestors to give you, blessing you with many children, numerous livestock, and abundant crops." (Deuteronomy 28:11 NLT)

"I will surely bless you and give you many descendants." (Romans 6:14 NIV)

"So numberless shall your descendants be!" (Romans 4:18 AMP)

"He rescues the poor who are godly, and gives them many children and much prosperity." (Psalm 107:41 TLB)

"The Lord will give you prosperity in the land He swore to your ancestors to give you, blessing you with many children." (Deuteronomy 28:11 NLT)

PART II

DEVOTIONALS

God is Doing Something New

"Forget the former things; do not dwell on the past. See, I am doing a new thing! Now it springs up; do you not perceive it?" Isaiah 43:18-19 NIV

The promise above has a special place in my heart. God has used it countless times to encourage me when I have experienced times of difficulty, disappointment, and despair. It has never failed to fill me with a fresh sense of hope whenever I read or hear it. Because of that, I often share it with people who write me for prayer and encouragement. These folks are usually looking for some glimmer of hope in a seemingly hopeless situation. Many times, they are hurting over some kind of heartbreak or loss, and they can't help but "dwell on the past" – what mistakes they might have made, and what they might have done differently to cause a better outcome. And even if the Lord is trying to do something new and wonderful in their lives or circumstances, they can't "perceive it" because they can't get past their past.

I had this very same problem myself over 40 years ago, when I experienced the first heartbreak of my young life. After being in a relationship with my high school sweetheart for more than three years, the relationship ended badly, and I felt the sting of rejection and betrayal. What I didn't realize at the time was that God wanted to do "a new thing" in my life, but He couldn't do that unless I got into agreement with

Him. As I look back, I marvel at the great lengths the Lord went to, in order to convince me that He had new plans for me that were better and brighter than I ever imagined.

First, he put my future husband, Joe, in the same college class with me in the Fall of 1973. And when months went by without Joe and I saying a word to each other, God had our professor put us in a skit together, so that we had to spend time with each other and work on our shared project. At the same time, the Lord arranged for Joe to buy a brand new Pontiac LeMans, knowing that my family and I always had Pontiacs, and that I wouldn't dream of saying 'no' when Joe offered to give me a ride in it. That day I rode in Joe's new car for the first time, he took me to lunch, and I told him my entire life story, even though I was usually a very private person. We had such a good time together that we both called our families and told them that we wouldn't be home for dinner that evening because we had other plans. After sharing another meal together that day, Joe declared that he was going to marry me. I laughed because it was so unexpected, but inwardly, his spontaneous expression of affection was exactly what my hurting heart needed – and the Lord knew it.

Looking back, I see now that God was working overtime to get me in agreement with His future plans for me, even where my choice of a lifemate was concerned. Truly, the similarities between us and our families were striking. Joe and I were both 100% Italian-American. All of the children in both families had first names starting with the letter "J". Both families had been buying and driving cars made by Pontiac for decades. Both of our fathers had served in the Air Force working on planes during World War II. And the list goes on and on. All of these things were God's way of trying to get me to stop dwelling on my past pain and disappointment, and to begin perceiving the new things He wanted to do in my life.

To this day, Joe and I laugh about how we sat in a classroom together for months, without knowing that our future spouse was so close at hand. And I am telling you all this today in the hope that you will be able to start believing that the "new thing" that God wants to do in YOUR life is closer than you think. Don't let how you perceive the past keep you from perceiving the bright and beautiful future that the Lord has for you. And don't think that your best days are behind you. God is still in the miracle-working business, and He loves transforming our troubles into triumphs. And right now, at this very moment, He's saying to you – "Forget about what's happened; don't keep going over old history. Be alert, be present. I'm about to do something brand-new. It's bursting out! Don't you see it? THERE IT IS!" (Isaiah 43:18-19 MSG)

Lord, open my eyes to the new and wonderful things You are longing to do in my life right now. Deliver me from the tendency to dwell on my past in ways that could hinder me from receiving the bright future You have for me. Cleanse my heart and mind of all bitterness, doubt, pain, and negativity. Show me signs that will move me to get into agreement with You and Your plans for my life. Help me to live a Christ-centered life so that I can experience the comfort, strength, and healing that only You can provide. Thank You that as I keep my hopes high, and my eyes of faith open, the "new things" You have for me will come bursting forth!

Promise-Power Point: God is continually leading His children into newer and better things, and if I will be sensitive to His voice and His vision for my life, nothing will be able to stop me from receiving the bright future He has for me.

Go in God's Strength

"I will go in the strength of the Lord God." Psalm 71:16 NKJV

The older I get, the more I realize how much I need to depend on God's strength. For example, when I have an appointment that I must go to that fills me with fear and dread, I know that this is my cue to practice relying on God's strength and power. The psalmist declared, "I will go in the strength of the Lord God." (Psalm 71:16 NKJV) This is the Word that the Holy Spirit often brings to my remembrance whenever I have to go somewhere I'd rather not go. There are a number of practical steps we can take in order to "go in the strength of the Lord."

First and foremost, we should spend some extra time in undistracted and unhurried prayer and Scripture reading. King David told God's people, "Seek the Lord; yes, seek His strength and seek His face untiringly." (1 Chronicles 16:11 TLB) David knew firsthand how important it was to continually seek God's face and strength. He won victory after victory, even when faced with overwhelming odds, because instead of relying on His own limited resources, He sought the Lord's power and strength. The Bible reveals that David often prayed for God's strength. "Look down in pity and grant strength to Your servant and save me." (Psalm 86:16 TLB) And we can do the same thing.

Meditating on, and declaring, God's Word and promises can also fill us with divine strength. "Never forget Your promises to me Your servant, for they are my only hope. They give me strength in all my troubles; how they refresh and revive me!" (Psalm 119:49-50 TLB) One of the problems with fear and dread is that they can cause us to lose our focus. Instead of keeping our eyes on God and His goodness, our focus can shift to all the things that we imagine could go wrong. Then it will be almost impossible to receive God's best in our situation. However, when we declare God's promises, the Spirit of God goes into action, and pours His strength and stability into us, and we are "refreshed and revived," as the Scripture says.

Worship and praise can energize us like nothing else can. So after we have prayed and claimed God's promises for our situation, we can imitate Abraham, and begin thanking the Lord in advance for a favorable outcome. "But Abraham never doubted. He believed God, for his faith and trust grew ever stronger, and he praised God for this blessing even before it happened. He was completely sure that God was well able to do anything He promised." (Romans 4:20-21 TLB) This is one way we can "walk by faith, and not by sight." (2 Corinthians 5:7 NKJV)

It's very helpful for us to get extra sleep the night before we have to keep an unpleasant appointment, especially if we have to get up early for it. "God wants His loved ones to get their proper rest." (Psalm 127:2 TLB) There are good reasons for the Lord wanting us to get the rest we need. When we are overtired or sleep-deprived, it can hinder our faith and our prayers. It can also cause us to treat people less kindly than we normally would. Peace will elude us, and our joy – which the Bible says is our strength – can evaporate. (Nehemiah 8:10) All these things can affect our outcome negatively, and it's simply not worth it.

Before I leave the house for an appointment I'm not looking forward to, I take out a tea bag and tea cup, and I set them on my kitchen counter next to my teapot. I begin to focus on some pleasant things I'm going to do when I get back home, and it brightens my outlook, and lifts my spirits. Perhaps right now, you are thinking of some appointments or events that you will be facing in the near future that are just begging for some divine strength. I urge you to begin preparing for them now, so that when the time comes, you can truly "go in the strength of the Lord God!"

Lord, when I am faced with things that fill me with fear or dread, teach me how to seek Your face and Your strength. Show me how to pray for the empowerment I need to accomplish all that You've called me to in this life. Make me devoted to Your Word and Your promises, and help me to use them to lay hold of everything You have in store for me. Remind me to praise and thank You in advance for the answers to my prayers. Thank You that as I rely on Your strength, my victory is assured!

Promise-Power Point: God will fill me with His own strength to go everywhere He sends me when I seek His face and His power through prayer, worship, and praise.

A Purpose for your Pain

"In the days to come you will understand all this."
Jeremiah 30:24 NLT

When our eight-year-old pet duck, Lily, became very ill, we took her to the vet and got her the medicines she needed to recover, and we earnestly prayed for her healing. We kept her and her mate, Larry, in our laundry room for two weeks, and we did our best to nurse Lily back to health. As she took a turn for the worse, my husband, Joe, looked in on her frequently as he worked at his computer in the next room. Then, it happened. Joe checked on Lily to see how she was doing and she looked at him, took her last breath, and died. Joe was inconsolable, and he asked me over and over, "Why would God allow me to see her take her last breath?" I did my best to comfort my husband, but I couldn't help asking myself the same thing. Why? Why would God allow this? It made no sense to me. Three years later, we got our answer.

Joe's mother was diagnosed with a terminal illness. We covered her in prayer each day, and she fought bravely to recover. When her doctors told her that there was nothing else they could do, she went into hospice care. Joe rushed to her side as her life ebbed away, and in the wee hours of the night, he saw his mother take her last breath. He was overcome with grief, but he felt upon Him the consoling hand of God as he remembered witnessing Lily's last breath of life. And he told me, "Now I understand."

All this brought to mind two different passages in the Bible where God tells the prophet Jeremiah, "In the days to come you will understand all this." (Jeremiah 30:24; 23:20) On both occasions, the Lord is telling Jeremiah about events to come, and He warns His servant that he won't be able to comprehend His purposes until they come to pass. In my husband's case, when God arranged for Joe to see Lily take her last breath, He was preparing him for witnessing his own mother's passing. It wasn't until it actually happened that he understood the Lord's purpose for his pain.

As Jesus was preparing to go to the cross, He told His disciples, "I still have many things to say to you, but you cannot bear them now." (John 16:12 NKJV) Can you imagine the Lord telling my husband, "I allowed you to experience the pain of seeing Lily take her last breath, so that you would be better prepared to see your mother die three years later"? Those are words that Joe was not prepared to hear at the time of Lily's death, and God knew it. So He allowed Joe to suffer with his questions and doubts for a time. And in the end, my husband had a deep-down peace and belief in God when he needed it most.

Perhaps you have questions and doubts of your own. I understand how you feel. But I'm asking you today to dare to believe that the Lord has a purpose for your pain, and to put your trust in Him while you wait for the revelations He has in store for you.

Lord, forgive me for doubting You and Your intentions when I have faced difficulties, disappointment, and heartache. Give me a trusting heart that believes that no matter what comes my way, You will work it all out for my good. (Romans 8:28) Help me to ask for Your comfort and healing when I need them. And teach me how to enjoy every day of my life right in the midst of trouble and turmoil. Thank You that as I keep my hope in You and Your promises, I will experience Your unshakable peace and unspeakable joy!

Promise-Power Point: When I truly believe that God has a purpose for my pain, I will find great peace and rest in the knowledge that He will reveal the worth and wisdom of His plans at the best possible time for me.

The Prayer of Agreement

"Again I tell you, if two of you on earth agree (harmonize together, make a symphony together) about whatever [anything and everything] they may ask, it will come to pass and be done for them by My Father in heaven." Matthew 18:19 AMP

Some months ago, I lost track of my car keys. It's not like me to lose track of something so important, so when it happened, it left me feeling frustrated and bewildered. I began praying about it right away, and after I poured out my heart to the Lord, I decided to ask one of my readers, Linda, to join her prayers with mine. Weeks passed, and I still had no idea where my car keys were. I thanked God that I had one spare set of keys, but with my husband, Joe, borrowing my car so much, I didn't feel secure about not having that original set. I continued to pray that God would restore my lost keys, but I must admit that my hope was fading. Every time I heard from Linda, she reassured me that she was still praying for the return of my keys, and that one day, they would show up. She never gave up hope, and she never stopped praying and sending me words of encouragement.

Weeks turned into months without any sign that my keys would ever be found. Then one day, I made an appointment at a beauty salon that I visit on occasion. When I walked through the door, the owner announced, "You left your car keys here the last time you came!" I was so thrilled with the good news that I didn't bother asking her why she didn't call me and let me know months ago that she had my missing keys. Besides, in my heart, I knew that God had a good reason for the incident, and that He had some lessons for me to learn.

This experience was a great reminder of the immeasurable power behind Christ's promise which says: "I tell you that if two of you on earth agree about anything you ask for, it will be done for you by My Father in heaven." (Matthew 18:19 NIV) I believe that if Christians really understood just how powerful the prayer of agreement can be, they would take advantage of it a lot more. Of course, WHO you ask to pray for you makes all the difference. It must be someone who has received Christ as their Savior, and who is considered "righteous" in His sight. (2 Corinthians 5:21) Scripture says: "The earnest (heartfelt, continued) prayer of a righteous man makes tremendous power available [dynamic in its working]." (James 5:16 AMP) When you ask a follower of Christ to pray in agreement with you according to the will of God, and when their petitions on your behalf are "heartfelt" and "continued," then you are truly blessed, and you will eventually see the answers to your prayers, if you don't lose hope. I especially like the Message Bible translation of James 5:16. "The prayer of a person living right with God is something powerful to be reckoned with." Even the devil himself cannot stand against the power of this kind of prayer.

The Scriptures reveal that the apostle Paul often asked other believers to pray for him. Though a great man of faith, he knew that there was simply no substitute for having others praying for him regularly. During a harrowing period of imprisonment, Paul wrote: "I am going to keep on being glad, for I know that as you pray for me, and as the Holy Spirit helps me, this is all going to turn out for my good." (Philippians 1:19 TLB) The great apostle made no qualms about having to depend on the Holy Spirit, and the prayers of fellow believers, to be able to rise above his circumstances, and to live out his faith in Christ. If Paul felt the need to ask his brothers and sisters in Christ for prayer on a regular basis, shouldn't you and I?

In Colossians, Paul talks about a fellow servant of Christ who was "always laboring earnestly in his prayers" for the believers, "that [they] may stand perfect and fully assured in all the will of God." (Colossians 4:12 NASB) My friend, Linda, is just such a person, as she is always ready and willing to pray for my needs, and the needs of my loved ones. And when the Lord blesses me as a result of her prayers, she is never jealous or envious. On the contrary, she is a perfect reflection of King David's joyful praises when he says: "We will sing for joy over your victory, and in the name of our God we will set up our banners. May the Lord fulfill all your petitions." (Psalm 20:5 NASB) Hallelujah!

If you don't have Christlike believers in your life who you can call upon for prayer at any time, I urge you to begin praying for some right now. Pray with confidence on the basis of God's promise in First John 5:14-15 (NIV), which says: "This is the confidence we have in approaching God: that if we ask anything according to His will, He hears us. And if we know that He hears us – whatever we ask – we know that we have what we asked of Him." And when the Lord sends these precious people into your life, treasure them, make the most of them, and be ready and willing to join your prayers with theirs in their time of need, just as they are always available to do the same for you!

Lord, thank You for the immeasurable power of the prayer of agreement. Teach me how to make the most of this privilege, and to use it to live a life that truly honors You. Bring fellow believers across my path who will joyfully "labor earnestly in prayer" for my needs and the needs of my loved ones. Make me willing to join my prayers with theirs for their own victories and blessings, and make me happy for them when their answers come. Today, I choose to persevere in prayer and in faith for the good things You have in store for me!

Promise-Power Point: **God has given me the privilege and responsibility to pray in agreement with other believers for His perfect will to come to pass in my life, and as I make the most of these rights, nothing and no one will be able to hinder me from receiving the answers to my prayers.**

Shunning Bitterness in Our Suffering

"Don't let your suffering embitter you at the only One who can deliver you." Job 36:18 TLB

I was thinking about some friends and loved ones who were going through some serious trials, when the Lord spoke to my heart and said, "If they just wouldn't get bitter, I could help them and heal them." You see, when we allow bitterness to creep into our hearts and minds, it cuts us off from the Person and power that we need the most in difficult times. Scripture warns us, "Don't let your suffering embitter you at the only One who can deliver you." (Job 36:18 TLB) I hear from people on a regular basis who are going through hard times, and I can tell by what they say that they have allowed bitterness to take root in their hearts by getting angry at God and His dealings with them. And it grieves my heart because I know that the way they respond to their trials will play a major part in their outcome.

Before I got serious about my relationship with the Lord many years ago, I never made the connection between how I responded to heartache and hardship, and my final outcome. Like most people, I thought that I could get angry and resentful, and even mistreat people, and still get the same results in the end. Often, I felt justified feeling sorry for myself, or holding grudges against others. I even thought that being mad at God was my personal right, when He allowed me to suffer more than I felt I deserved. I didn't realize that I was not leaving room for the Lord to work mightily on my behalf whenever I responded wrongly to my trials.

After I surrendered my life to the Lord for real those many years ago, I began an in-depth study of the Bible. That's when I discovered that while my bitterness was not giving God the opportunity to act on my behalf, it WAS giving Satan and his dark forces an open door to my life and my circumstances. The apostle Paul wrote: "When angry, do not sin; do not ever let your wrath (your exasperation, your fury or indignation) last until the sun goes down. Leave no [such] room or foothold for the devil [give no opportunity to him]." (Ephesians 4:26-27 AMP) And as I gave the devil permission to destroy my life through my bitterness and unforgiveness, I experienced more and more troubles, and drifted further from the Lord and His good plans for me.

God has taught me that when His people go through difficult times, our perspective and focus are crucial. That's one reason why the author of Hebrews wrote that we should constantly be "Looking away [from all that will distract] to Jesus, Who...for the joy [of obtaining the prize] that was set before Him, endured the cross, despising and ignoring the shame, and is now seated at the right hand of the throne of God. Just think of Him Who endured from sinners such grievous opposition and bitter hostility against Himself [reckon up and consider it all in comparison with your trials], so that you may not grow weary or exhausted, losing heart and relaxing and fainting in your minds." (Hebrews 12:2-3 AMP) Jesus is our example for living our lives on this earth, and if we ask for His perspective on our circumstances, and compare our trials with His, we will begin to see things through His eyes, and we will have all the power and wisdom we need to respond in a Christlike manner. And exemplifying Christ in our situation will enable us to lay hold of all the blessings, rewards, and victories God has in store for those who honor and obey Him.

If you are a believer like me, and people around you know it, then sooner or later, when those folks are going through trying times, they are going to hit you with some challenging questions about God. Why is this happening to me? What kind of God allows people to suffer like this? And on and on. The apostle Peter has some advice for you and me in times like these. "But in your hearts revere Christ as Lord. Always be prepared to give an answer to everyone who asks you to give the reason for the hope that you have. But do this with gentleness and respect, keeping a clear conscience, so that those who speak maliciously against your good behavior in Christ may be ashamed of their slander." (1 Peter 3:15-16 NIV) God will give you the right words at the right time to speak words of wisdom, truth, and encouragement to these people, if you ask Him to. And you will have planted seeds of hope in their hearts that can ultimately change their lives and draw them to Christ.

Jesus declared, "Blessed is the one who does not lose his faith in Me." (Luke 7:23 TLB) There are extraordinary blessings awaiting the believer who refuses to allow doubt, discouragement, and bitterness to rob them of their inheritance in Christ. Are you ready to give God the opportunity to show Himself strong in your life and circumstances today?

Lord, when trouble comes my way, help me to respond in a Christlike manner – full of faith, forgiveness, and hope. Guard me from the bitterness, resentment, and self-pity that can open the door to the forces of darkness whose only purpose is to steal, kill, and destroy. (John 10:10) Remind me often that how I respond to hardship and heartache will play a major part in my final outcome. Thank You that as I keep my eyes on You, and trust You to work everything out for my good – including my trials – You will bless me and use me in new and exciting ways for Your glory! (Romans 8:28)

Promise-Power Point: The Lord will reward me with extraordinary blessings and victories when I face adverse circumstances without bitterness, resentment, or doubt.

The Lord Remembers Us

"The Lord remembers us and will bless us." Psalm 115:12 NIV

Forty-one years ago, before my husband, Joe, and I were married, I was having dinner with him and his family in their home. After we finished eating, we all got up and began clearing away the dishes, and straightening up the kitchen. As I passed Joe's parents' bedroom, I noticed a beautifully-carved wooden cross hanging on the wall over their bed. I had never seen anything like it, and as I remarked on its stunning appearance, my mother-in-law told me that she would like me to have it after she was gone. I was deeply touched, and as I began thanking her, her daughter insisted that she would like to have it as her own, and we left it at that.

Years went by, and my in-laws moved hundreds of miles away. Then Joe's dad passed away, and my sister-in-law moved in with her mother. Last week, my husband was at his mother's bedside when she took her last breath. He was thankful that he was able to be there for her, but her passing left a terrible ache in his heart. Since Joe is the oldest child in his family, he took on the big brother role and did his best to comfort and console his younger siblings. After making the proper funeral arrangements, the siblings decided to meet at their mother's house to decide the fate of her belongings. Joe told his loved ones that they could have everything that their mom left behind. Then he spotted the wooden cross above his mother's bed. He took it in his hands and announced that he would like to have it. And the same sister who claimed it as her own forty-one years ago declared that he was welcomed to it.

After Joe arrived home that weekend after a long and exhausting drive, he unpacked his car and showed me his parents' cross. I was stunned and speechless. He asked what was wrong, and I told him about the conversation his mom and I had over 41 years ago. Joe didn't remember how much that cross meant to me, but the Lord did. And at a time when I was filled with sorrow and grief, He sent me a precious gift to ease my pain and heartache. My in-laws' cross hangs on our bedroom wall now, and every time that Joe and I see it, we are reminded not only of his parents, but of a loving God who remembers us and blesses us when we need it most.

Scripture says, "The Lord remembers us and will bless us." (Psalm 115:12 NIV) Perhaps your life hasn't turned out quite like you planned, and you are feeling forsaken and forgotten. Even if others have forgotten you, rest assured that the Lord not only remembers you, but He also remembers your dreams and desires. And if you keep your faith in Him, and live your life for Him, the day will come when His gifts and blessings suddenly show up. Let me encourage you to begin confessing with confidence every day, "The Lord remembers me and He will bless me!"

Lord, fill me with a Christlike confidence that will enable me to trust and believe You for all the good things You have in store for me. When doubts begin to assail me, help me to spend extra time in Your presence and Your Word, feeding on Your promises. Teach me how to resist and rebuke self-pity, bitterness, and sorrow. Help me to focus on all the good things in my life. Give me a tender heart and a tender conscience, so that I won't have to forfeit or delay Your blessings. Thank You that You will never forget or forsake me!

Promise-Power Point: No matter how things look, I know in my heart that the Lord remembers me and will bless me, as I choose to continually seek and serve Him, and trust in His goodness and faithfulness.

Faith Failures

"You of little faith," He said, "why did you doubt?"
Matthew 14:31 NIV

I really appreciate how willing the Lord is to instruct us and tell us what changes we need to make when we seek Him about a concern or problem we have. In my case, I had begun getting sick a lot lately, and the whole thing had me confused and discouraged. At first, I made assumptions about it that didn't do a thing to solve my problem. When I got a nudge from the Holy Spirit to take the time to have a heart-to-heart talk with the Lord about it, I finally began to get some solid answers.

The first thing God told me was that I had caused my resistance to get low by depriving myself of the kind of sleep that my body and mind needed most. He reminded me of the Scripture that says, "God wants His loved ones to get their proper rest." (Psalm 127:2 TLB) The truth is that no matter how important we think our work is, or how much others depend on us, it is never God's will for us to let ourselves get run down. Whenever we begin depriving ourselves of the rest and restoration we need on a daily basis, our priorities are wrong somehow. If we will go to the Lord and ask for His help and guidance, He will show us what changes we need to make, and He will help us to follow His lead as we look to Him every step of the way. And our bodies, and our health, will thank us for it.

The Lord also showed me that one of the reasons for the attacks on my health was that I wasn't confessing His Word as diligently as I used to, and I was experiencing a major faith failure. Scripture tells us that hearing the Word of God increases our faith. (Romans 10:17) And hearing ourselves declare God's Word and promises over and over is one of the quickest and best ways to build our faith, even faith for healing and wholeness. The apostle Paul wrote, "And now I entrust you to God and His care and to His wonderful words which are able to build your faith and give you all the inheritance of those who are set apart for Himself." (Acts 20:32 TLB)

When your faith is faltering, the most powerful thing you can do is to begin confessing the promises of God that pertain to your situation. God's Word has the power to not only build and boost our faith, but to renew our minds. And according to Scripture, we can't know the perfect will of God, or receive everything He has for us, until our minds are properly renewed. "Do not be conformed to this world (this age), [fashioned after and adapted to its external, superficial customs], but be transformed (changed) by the [entire] renewal of your mind [by its new ideals and its new attitude], so that you may prove [for yourselves] what is the good and acceptable and perfect will of God, even the thing which is good and acceptable and perfect [in His sight for YOU]." (Romans 12:2 AMP) Either our hearts and minds will be programmed by the world, or by the Word. If by the world, we will get all the misery and mediocrity that the world has to offer. If by the Word, we will experience the abundant life that Jesus died to give us. (John 10:10)

The Lord also revealed to me that I had become an easy target for the devil and his dark forces by focusing too much on the disappointments in my life and in my work, and by yielding to discouragement, instead of resisting it. I once heard someone wisely say that disappointment is inevitable, while discouragement is a choice. We live in a fallen world filled with broken people, so we can't always avoid disappointments. Loved ones we thought we could count on will let us down. Our work will not always bring us the satisfaction, recognition, or reward that we had hoped for. And at times, our lives will not seem fulfilling or meaningful. But when we bring our disappointments and heartaches to the Lord in honest, unedited prayers, He will enable us to see ourselves and our circumstances from His perspective, and He will cause our problems to profit us somehow, just like He promised. (Romans 8:28)

The most important thing I learned from this experience is that if we are not constantly alert and vigilant, we can allow doubt and unbelief to creep into our minds and hearts. Excessive fatigue, failure to confess God's Word, and giving place to discouragement can all render our faith ineffective. When that happens, we lose our most intimate connection to the Lord, along with His mightiest interventions and richest blessings. Could you be experiencing a faith failure of your own today?

Lord, I regret the times I allowed doubt and unbelief to hamper my faith out of laziness or negligence. Show me how to get the proper rest and relaxation every day, and to strike the perfect balance between work and play. I don't want to be driven by selfish ambition or worldly pursuits, but led by Your Spirit at all times. Remind me that discouragement can be highly destructive, and to take it seriously, so that I can be quick to resist it and refuse it. Fill me with a growing passion for Your Word, so that I can use it as an "indispensable weapon" against the dark forces. (Ephesians 6:17 MSG) Thank You that as I partner with You for the building of my faith, doubt and unbelief will not be able to rob me of Your very best blessings!

Promise-Power Point: God will make me invulnerable to faith failures as I refuse to become too tired, too negligent of the Word, or too discouraged.

Peace and Effective Prayer

"Do not be anxious about anything, but in every situation, by prayer and petition, with thanksgiving, present your requests to God. And the peace of God, which transcends all understanding, will guard your hearts and your minds in Christ Jesus." Philippians 4:6-7 NIV

I was ministering to a dear lady the other day whose husband has been suffering from a debilitating disease the last few years. She shared with me how difficult it has been for her to watch her loved one's health deteriorating, and to bear the burden of having to perform more and more of his daily tasks, as well as her own. I had great compassion for this woman because I had watched my own husband, Joe, suffer with some very serious afflictions over the years. At the age of 51, he suffered a massive heart attack that nearly took his life. Several years later, he needed open-heart surgery to repair a valve that was rapidly failing. Within the last few months, Joe has received two new diagnoses of diseases that initially left us stunned and disheartened. But you know what? I continue to pray and claim God's promises of healing, health, and wholeness for myself and my loved ones daily, with just as much hope and enthusiasm as I ever did.

You see, as I sought the Lord for His wisdom and guidance about my husband's latest health challenges, He reminded me about an experience I had with a friend some years ago. I was lamenting to her how my 4-year-old pet duck, Larry, had been diagnosed with severe arthritis in his legs. He was having trouble walking, and it was heartbreaking watching him trying to keep up with our other ducks. Lameness in a duck can be very serious, even life-threatening, so I knew that this diagnosis of arthritis could be a death sentence for him. As I described my feelings of disappointment and sadness to my friend, she told me, "Enjoy every single day that you have Larry. See him as a precious gift from the Lord, and keep thanking God for him." I am happy to report that I took her words to heart, and that Larry will be celebrating his 15th birthday this summer.

The Lord was reminding me about my friend's "prescription" for adjusting my focus in a difficult situation, because He wanted to bring to my remembrance some of the most powerful principles in His Word. "Do not be anxious about anything, but in every situation, by prayer and petition, with thanksgiving, present your requests to God. And the peace of God, which transcends all understanding, will guard your hearts and your minds in Christ Jesus." (Philippians 4:6-7 NIV) I had read these verses of Scripture countless times over the years, but I always seemed to focus more on the "prayer and petition" part, than the "thanksgiving" part. And because of that, I had often continued to fret and worry about something that was troubling me. But since I have learned to have an attitude of gratitude in challenging situations, I have experienced more peace and stability than I ever dreamed possible. I have discovered that the more I give thanks, the more peace I have. And the more peace I have, the more effective my prayers are. In other words, my faith works better when I am at peace.

The Bible says, "The effective prayer of a righteous man can accomplish much." (James 5:16 NASB) There are effective prayers, and then there are ineffective prayers. The Scripture promises that when our prayers are effective, they can accomplish great things. When our focus and perspective are right when we pray – when we are not fretting, fuming, or fearful when we pray – we can see God Almighty move heaven and earth on our behalf.

Nowadays, whenever I am tempted to worry or think negatively about my husband's health problems, I begin thanking and praising the Lord that Joe is in my life, and I appreciate our time together more and more. Perhaps you or your loved ones are facing some daunting circumstances of your own today, and you are wondering if your life will ever be the same. I believe I know how you feel, dear one. And I tell you now that if you will seek God's face with all your heart, and call on Him with a sense of gratitude and humility, He will sustain you with His perfect peace while you wait on Him to do what only He can do!

Lord, teach me how to pray effective prayers for myself and my loved ones. Help me to cooperate with You for the building of my faith. Give me a growing passion for Your presence and Your Word. Show me how to pray and stand on Your promises in every situation. Thank You that as I choose to give thanks for all the good in my life, You will fill me with Your peace, and bring Your promises to pass!

Promise-Power Point: Since God loves and responds to a grateful heart, I will have His peace in the midst of trouble, and see Him work mightily on my behalf, when I continually give Him thanks and praise.

Share Their Joy

"Do not merely look out for your own personal interests, but also for the interests of others."
Philippians 2:4 NASB

A dear friend of mine was telling me all about her upcoming vacation plans when I got a twinge of envy and self-pity deep inside of me. My husband, Joe, and I haven't had a real vacation in over 15 years, since we began raising ducks as pets. It can be challenging enough to find someone trustworthy to care for your dog or cat while you're away, but have you ever tried to get a duck sitter? As I listened to my friend gushing about her getaway plans, the Spirit of God spoke to my heart and urged me to be genuinely happy for her. He reminded me of the Lord's instructions in Philippians 2:4 (TLB), "Don't just think about your own affairs, but be interested in others, too, and in what they are doing." Right then and there, I made a decision to push my feelings aside, and to be sincerely happy for my friend's blessings and interests. That's when I began to sense supernatural joy and peace springing up on the inside of me.

As I did a little soul-searching during our conversation, I realized that Joe and I were in a season of our lives where we were enjoying and benefiting immensely from having pet ducks. Since Joe and I are in our 60s now, I know that we are getting closer to a time when having pets like these will no longer be practical or desirable for us. So for now, I want to appreciate and embrace this precious season of our lives so that when it finally comes to an end, I will take comfort in the knowledge that I made the most of it.

I have to say that it's very common for me to run into folks who are blatantly jealous of other people's vacations and blessings. And many of these people are Christians. While it can be "natural" for us to initially be a bit envious of others when they describe their good fortune, believers have the ability and responsibility through the power of God's Spirit to "switch gears," and to choose to be genuinely happy for others in these situations. You and I don't have to bow down to our feelings. In every situation, we have the power to choose joy. To choose peace. To choose contentment. To choose gratitude. And especially, to choose to love as Jesus does.

Scripture tells us to "Rejoice with those who rejoice [sharing others' joy], and weep with those who weep [sharing others' grief]." (Romans 12:15 AMP) When we hear of others' blessings, the Lord wants us to "share their joy". We can't do that if we're feeling jealous or envious. Only by sharing their joy can we sow good seeds that will enable us to reap a harvest of blessings for ourselves in the days ahead. Solomon wrote: "A calm and undisturbed mind and heart are the life and health of the body, but envy, jealousy, and wrath are like rottenness of the bones." (Proverbs 14:30 AMP) How we view, treat, and speak of others will affect every part of us, including our minds, hearts, and bodies. Our thoughts, attitudes, and actions can minister life and health to every fiber of our being when we are following the Holy Spirit's lead. On the other hand, when we choose disobedience over God's way, we could be ministering death and destruction to ourselves. Proverbs 11:17 (NLT) says, "Those who are kind benefit themselves, but the cruel bring ruin on themselves." Don't be fooled into thinking that how you relate to others won't affect your own well-being.

Maybe you haven't had a decent vacation in years, and you are surrounded by people who are enjoying them regularly. Or perhaps you are driving an old beat-up car, and you keep encountering those who can buy new vehicles every few years. Instead of giving in to jealousy or despair, determine to sow good seed by sharing their joy. As you do, take comfort in the fact that your harvest of blessings is on its way to you!

Lord, forgive me for the times that I failed to take an interest in others and what they were doing, and I chose to focus on myself and my own interests instead. Work in my heart and my mind so that I can be more Christlike in my thoughts, feelings, and attitudes. Teach me how to be genuinely happy for people when they are enjoying things that are out of my reach. When I am tempted to become jealous or envious, remind me of how I could be harming my health and well-being. Thank You that as I rejoice with those who rejoice, and share their joy, I will experience the abundant life and blessing that You promise in Your Word!

Promise-Power Point: God's will for me is to take a genuine interest in what others are doing, and to be genuinely joyful for them, so that I can avoid the bitter harvest that a jealous spirit reaps, and instead enjoy the harvest of blessings that belong to a Christlike child of God.

Preserving Our Families

"A wise woman builds her home, but a foolish woman tears it down with her own hands." Proverbs 14:1 NLT

It wasn't all that long ago that my family and I had a lovely couple living next door that we enjoyed having in our neighborhood. Dan and Margie seemed so happily married and so much in love. They had no children of their own, but they had many relatives with children who often allowed their kids to stay with Dan and Margie, sometimes for weeks. After a while, Dan began complaining to my husband, Joe, that Margie was giving all of her attention to the children who were staying with them, and very little to him. Joe took Margie aside and tried explaining to her how neglected Dan was feeling, and he gave her a friendly warning. When Margie showed no signs of changing her behavior, I gave her a friendly warning of my own. Dan was a very kind and understanding man, but I knew that everyone had their limits, and I didn't want to see their marriage torn apart because of Margie's thoughtless and reckless behavior. Things got so bad that Dan eventually walked out on Margie and their marriage. It was then that Margie realized how foolish she had been, but it was too late. Dan was gone for good, and there was nothing she could do about it. She sank into a pit of depression and tried to kill herself. Sometime later, she moved out of our neighborhood, and we heard through one of our other neighbors some months later that she had died.

Whenever I think of this sad story, I can't help thinking of Solomon's proverb which says, "A wise woman builds her home, but a foolish woman tears it down with her own hands." (Proverbs 14:1 NLT) Margie had been a very fortunate woman. She had a husband who loved her and was devoted to her. Instead of appreciating him and listening to his concerns and complaints, she foolishly gave her own needs and desires so much importance that she forgot about those of her husband, and eventually forfeited her marriage. The only consolation that Joe and I had was that we had repeatedly tried to warn Margie that she was on dangerous ground. If she had taken our warnings to heart, and approached her husband with humility and remorse, she could have saved her marriage, and spared herself a lot of misery. Instead, a good marriage came to an abrupt end, and so did Margie's life.

I know how difficult it can be to keep a marriage and family together, because my husband and I have been married for 40 years. We have had our share of trouble and trials, and we have experienced periods of resentment, unforgiveness, and strife. Together, we have faced unbearable sorrow, regret, and disappointment. And there have been many times we were tempted to walk away from each other, but we resisted. And it has paid off. I will be honest with you and share with you here one of the things that has helped me to persevere in difficult times where my marriage is concerned. Years ago, after my high school sweetheart abruptly ended our three-year relationship, I was devastated. I couldn't accept that it was over, and that I had to move on. I kept trying to convince my boyfriend that we belonged together, to no avail. Eventually, I got the message, and I met my husband, Joe, in one of my college classes. Then it was my boyfriend who expressed a desire for us to reconcile. When I told him that it was too late, he confessed that he was haunted by memories of me trying to get back together. Because I never wanted to make the same mistake that he did, I have always thought twice about walking out on my marriage, even in the most difficult of times. And I thank God that I had that experience so many years ago, and that I learned from it.

Marriages and families can be fragile. We live in a cold and broken world. Besides that, the devil and his dark forces continually work overtime to try to destroy our families. You and I have to be very careful not to tear down our households with our own hands. With God's help, we can be ever watchful and alert to attacks on our families, and we can neutralize them with prayer and obedience to God's laws and biblical principles. Are you prepared to fight for your family?

Lord, today, I want to thank You for my loved ones. I commit them and myself to You, and I ask that You fill us with the love, respect, humility, and wisdom we need to make our house the kind of home that will be like heaven on earth. Most of all, instill in us a holy reverence for You and Your Word, and teach us how to love each other with Your kind of love. Guard us from the kind of selfishness and strife that can tear us apart, and make us quick to forgive each other with all our hearts. Thank You that as we live lives that honor You, and consider each other's welfare as much as our own, You will preserve and prosper our family!

Promise-Power Point: God is willing to protect my home and family, and to cause them to thrive, when I do my part to live in peace, harmony, and unity with my loved ones.

Radical Blessing

"Let the LORD *be magnified, who delights and takes pleasure in the prosperity of His servant." Psalm 35:27 AMP*

Last week, my son, John, injured his right thumb at work. Since his wife, Amy, is an operating room nurse, she promptly got an appointment for John with a surgeon that she knows and respects. When the surgeon examined the injured thumb, he determined that it was badly damaged and infected, and that it required surgery as soon as possible. He was prepared to do the operation right then and there, but my son had misgivings about the procedure, and he asked for an appointment for the following week. When I found out about all this, I immediately turned to the Lord and began praying that He would heal John's thumb without surgery. I asked God to do such a perfect work of healing in my son that the next time the surgeon examined him, he would accurately and honestly say that the thumb looked so good that surgery would not be necessary. Today was the day that John was scheduled for surgery, and I am praising and thanking God because He answered my prayers for my son exactly as I had prayed them. Upon examining John's injured thumb this morning, the surgeon declared that my son's wound and infection were completely healed, and there was absolutely no need for surgery.

As I was expressing my heartfelt thanks to the Lord for the answers to my prayers, He revealed to me that He did not rescue my son simply because he was my son. But He did it mainly because John is a devoted servant of His. He reminded me of His Word in Psalm 35:27 (NIV) which says: "The Lord be exalted, who delights in the well-being of His servant." The Lord showed me that when I ask Him for deliverance and blessings for those who are devoted to Him, I can go ahead and pray for – and expect – radical answers to my prayers. He also showed me that I should not beat myself up when I pray for people who aren't seeking Him or serving Him, and I don't get the results I had hoped for. I must confess that I absolutely love praying for my brothers and sisters in Christ, especially for those who are living for Him instead of themselves, because I know that God is eager to bless their obedience in extraordinary ways. And when I join my faith with theirs, anything can happen.

If you're wondering what a true servant of the Lord looks like, all you need to do is read the first psalm in the Bible. "Oh, the joys of those who do not follow evil men's advice, who do not hang around with sinners, scoffing at the things of God. But they delight in doing everything God wants them to, and day and night are always meditating on His laws and thinking about ways to follow Him more closely." (Psalm 1:1-2 TLB) If these verses describe you, then you can confidently pray radical prayers for yourself, and expect the Lord to do "exceedingly abundantly" above all you ask or think.

(Ephesians 3:20 NKJV) If these verses don't fit you right now, then I urge you to get busy seeking and serving God the way He desires and deserves. He will show you how to do it, if you ask Him to.

Scripture says: "The LORD favors those who fear and worship Him [with awe-inspired reverence and obedience], those who wait for His mercy and lovingkindness." (Psalm 147:11 AMP) God's love is unconditional. But His favor, blessings, and rewards are not. Those who demonstrate genuine fear and reverence for the Lord and His Word by their obedience will experience answers to their prayers that doubtful, disobedient Christians will not. We are living in dangerous times. Lines are being drawn. The devil knows his time is short, and he and his evil cohorts are working overtime to lead people away from God and His laws, principles, and truths. Don't you be one of his casualties.

Lord, make me a true servant of Yours – one who demonstrates genuine fear and reverence for You and Your laws through my thoughts, words, and actions. Cleanse my heart and mind of everything that is not of You. Deliver me from all doubt and unbelief that would keep me out of Your will, and make me vulnerable to satanic attack. Make me a lover and doer of Your Word, and help me to cooperate with You for the building of my faith. Thank You that as I follow You in wholehearted obedience, I can expect radical answers to my prayers!

Promise-Power Point: God holds in store extraordinary blessings and rewards for His devoted servants, and as I determine to obey Him in my character, conduct, and conversation, I will see Him work wonders on my behalf.

Pray for All People

"I urge you, first of all, to pray for all people. Ask God to help them; intercede on their behalf, and give thanks for them. This is good and pleases God our Savior, who wants everyone to be saved and to understand the truth." 1 Timothy 2:1,3-4 NLT

My husband, Joe, and I were in our car on the way to do some errands one Saturday, when an aggressive driver suddenly cut my husband off, nearly causing an accident. Joe was furious and began calling the other driver some unflattering names, even though the other car was already out of sight. When I suggested that Joe pray for the other person, he got indignant and said that he had no intention of doing so. I totally understood my husband's attitude, and I silently lifted the other driver up in prayer to the Lord.

The reason why I understood my husband's refusal to pray for that reckless driver is that many years ago, it never occurred to me to pray for someone I didn't know, let alone someone who had offended me, or tried to hurt me. But once I made a quality decision to get serious about my relationship with the Lord, I discovered in His Word that His will is for me to pray for everyone. Scripture says: "I urge you, first of all, to pray for all people. Ask God to help them; intercede on their behalf, and give thanks for them. This is good and pleases God our Savior, who wants everyone to be saved and to understand the truth." (1 Timothy 2:1,3-4

NLT) One reason why the Lord didn't take you and me to heaven as soon as we received Christ as our Savior, and accepted His precious gift of salvation, is that He wants to use us while we are here to impact the lives of countless people that we come in contact with. One way that we can make an eternal difference in someone's life is to pray for them. God wants us to take seriously the promise He made to us in James 5:16 (NIV): "The prayer of a righteous person is powerful and effective."

The truth is that sometimes, when we are waiting for the Lord to act on our behalf in some way, He is actually waiting on us to pray for those who are involved in our situation. And when we do that, we are "pleasing God," as the above Scripture says, and He will reward us for it by working in our lives and circumstances. Perhaps you are wondering how you can pray for people that you don't even know. If we use the verses above as a guide, we can "ask God to help them," and we can pray that they would "be saved and understand the truth". The Lord has promised that when we ask Him for anything in line with His will, we can be confident that our prayers will be answered. So we have His assurance that He will honor our prayers on behalf of these people. (1 John 5:14-15)

I believe that sometimes, God allows us to become involved in "sticky" situations simply because He wants us to pray for the people these situations will put us in touch with. If we respond to these challenges in ways that please and honor God, we will receive blessings, rewards, and opportunities that we couldn't receive any other way. These are the times when we can claim and lean heavily upon His promise which says that He will work all things together for our good. (Romans 8:28) And the more we cooperate with His will and purposes for our problems, the more benefits we will reap from them in the end.

When we have troubles of our own and pray for others, it helps to take our focus off of ourselves and our problems, and it shifts our focus to others and their concerns. We may never know how burdened people we pray for might be. Some of them will surely be facing some downright scary circumstances. Some of these folks will have no one to pray for them. Some may be suicidal or self-destructive. And some of them may be on their way to hell. Our prayers may be the only thing that stand between them and certain doom. It's for these reasons that I have made it my business to pray for everyone I come in contact with – in person, through the internet, by telephone, or any other way. I pray for my doctors and their staff members, as well as for their families. I pray for the companies I patronize, along with all their people. When I go shopping, I pray for the stores I visit, as well as for their employees. And when I go to a restaurant, I not only pray for favor for excellent seating and service, but I pray for everyone there, asking the Lord to make Himself real to them in life-changing ways. I'm not talking about praying pitiful prayers for these people. I'm talking about prayers that make a real difference in their lives.

Maybe it never occurred to you that your outcome in a situation could depend upon you praying for the people involved. But since the Bible says that real faith works through love, praying for those you come in contact with in any given situation can activate the power of God to move mountains on your behalf. (Galatians 5:6; Mark 11:22-24) Today, I challenge you to put these powerful biblical principles to work in your life, and open the door for God to reveal Himself to you – and those you pray for – in life-changing ways!

Lord, remind me often that You tell us in Your Word to "pray for all people". Lead me to pray for You to "help them," but most of all, direct me to pray that they will "be saved and understand the truth". Guard me from the bitterness, resentment, and pride that would hinder me from praying for those who hurt or offend me. And remind me that Jesus commands us to bless and pray for our worst enemies. (Matthew 5:43-45; Luke 6:27-28) Thank You that as I exercise my faith by interceding for others, You will reward me with supernatural peace, joy, and blessings of every kind!

Promise-Power Point: *As a servant of Christ, I am called to pray for those I come in contact with in my daily life, and as I obey Him in this area, I will witness Him working mightily in my life, and in the lives of others, for all eternity.*

The Fear of Human Opinion

"The fear of human opinion disables; trusting God protects you from that." Proverbs 29:25 MSG

When my husband, Joe, and I moved into our home in Eastern Pennsylvania years ago, there were curtains on our front picture window that I really liked. They were a pretty "balloon" style, and they were printed with beautiful little roses all over. They complemented our living room wallpaper perfectly, and I decided that we would keep them. Then one of my longtime friends came over to see our new home. She looked all around our house, and she seemed pleasantly surprised at how nicely decorated it was. But to my dismay, she didn't say a word about my picture window curtains. After she left, I took a closer look at the curtains and noticed that they were faded in some spots. I even noticed some areas that looked worn and frayed. And I began thinking to myself, "My friend didn't like these curtains, with good reason. They look old, and they don't go well with the décor." Then I set about making plans to replace them.

With Joe's help, I measured the window, and ordered custom-made vertical blinds in a color that would go well with our furniture and carpeting. I was sorry to see my flowery curtains go, but I kept telling myself that the new blinds would be a big improvement. The next time my friend came over, she noticed our new blinds and declared, "What happened to the lovely flowery balloon curtains you had hanging in the front window the last time I came? I had never seen such a beautiful window treatment before." My heart sank. I had convinced myself that my friend didn't like those curtains – even though I loved them myself – and I had taken them down and thrown them out, simply because I thought that she didn't approve of them.

Even though this incident happened many years ago, the Spirit of God often brings it to my remembrance when I begin worrying too much about what other people think. It's a habit that most people practice, even though they aren't always aware of it. And Satan and his minions use it as a weapon against us, to discourage us and get us out of the will of God. Solomon wrote, "Fearing people is a dangerous trap, but trusting the Lord means safety." (Proverbs 29:25 NLT) Why is being too concerned about what other people think a "dangerous trap"? Because instead of consulting the Lord about a matter, and following the leading of the Holy Spirit, we will be led by what other people say and think, and we will miss out on the divine solutions, opportunities, and rewards that God had in store for us.

As Christians, we are called to follow in the footsteps of our Savior, Jesus, who said, "I do nothing without consulting the Father." (John 5:30 NLT) If the Son of God lived His life in total dependence upon the Father, how much more should we! Unfortunately, many believers think that God isn't interested in the small details of their lives, and the trouble with this kind of mindset is that what started out as a minor issue or dilemma, often turns into a major problem. David wrote: "The Lord directs the steps of the godly. He delights in every detail of their lives. Though they stumble, they will never fall, for the Lord holds them by the hand." (Psalm 37:23-24 NLT) When we have the attitude that God wants to be involved in "every detail" of our lives – and consult Him in small matters, as well as in larger ones – even if we "stumble" and make a mistake, He will keep a tight grip on us, and make sure we don't "fall" to our destruction.

That day, when I assumed that my friend didn't like my original living room curtains, I threw away something I treasured. I cared more about her opinion than I did my own, and it cost me. These days, when I find myself in a similar situation, I search my own heart for how I feel, and I consult God for His perspective in the matter. I often pray, "What do YOU have to say about this, Lord?" And I listen intently for His voice, doing my best to follow His lead. I promise you that if you use the same strategy, you will save yourself a lot of trouble, disappointment, time – and money!

Lord, forgive me for "fearing people," and caring more about their opinions than Yours, or my own. Ground me in Your love and truth, and guard me from feelings of insecurity and poor self-esteem that can cause me to make foolish and hasty decisions that I will regret later on. Help me to live a Christ-centered life, and teach me how to consult You about all the things You want me to. Work in my heart and mind so that I will truly believe that You always want what is best for me. Thank You that as I do my best to follow the leading of Your Spirit, I will experience the blessed freedom and rewards that belong to me in Christ!

Promise-Power Point: *When I resist caring about human opinions that conflict with God's will for me – consulting Him, and trusting Him all the way – He will reward me by protecting me and prospering me.*

The Consequences of Loose Talk

"Loose talk has a way of getting picked up and spread around. Little birds drop the crumbs of your gossip far and wide." Ecclesiastes 10:20 MSG

The verse above from the Message Bible is a clear warning to those of us who make careless and bitter remarks about others, thinking that they will never reach the ears of those they are leveled against. I heard from just such a woman recently, who was lamenting over the strife and division in her household because of some comments she had made about one family member in the presence of another family member, who relayed those comments to the target of her criticism. Here it was seven years later, and the victim of her bitter words still had not forgiven her, and as a result, the entire family was divided. Each time a special occasion or celebration was planned for the family, this woman was pointedly left out, and she was reminded yet again of her careless and thoughtless words against her relative.

Solomon wrote: "Do not revile the king even in your thoughts, or curse the rich in your bedroom, because a bird in the sky may carry your words, and a bird on the wing may report what you say." (Ecclesiastes 10:20 NIV) Sometimes, when you ask someone how they discovered a secret of yours, they may respond with, "A little bird told me." That's because our words have a way of being spread around even when we never meant them to be. Jesus told His disciples: "There is nothing concealed that will not be disclosed, or hidden that will not be made known. What you have said in the dark will be heard in the daylight, and what you have whispered in the ear in the inner rooms will be proclaimed from the roofs." (Luke 12:2-3 NIV) The Master's words should fill us with a healthy fear of God where our conversation is concerned. If we remember that the Lord hears every word we say, we will be less casual with our speech, and we will carefully consider what the consequences for our words might be down the line. There's an old saying that says, "You can't un-ring a bell." Once a sound is released into the atmosphere, it can't be taken back. The same is true for the words we speak.

Suppose instead of being the ones who are gossiping, you and I are on the listening end of gossipy speech? We can make a decision then and there that we are not going to spread the bitter words by repeating them to others. When my husband, Joe, and I were getting Christian counseling in the early years of our marriage, we got some of the best advice we have ever had. Each time we described occasions of strife or gossip in our extended families, our counselor would say, "Don't feed into that!" As we refused to engage in divisive and bitter conduct and speech with our family members, Joe and I had more peace and joy than ever before, and our marriage got stronger and healthier. Today, we have been married for forty years, and our relationship continues to improve as we apply more and more biblical principles to our daily living. Scripture says: "Without wood a fire goes out; without gossip a quarrel dies down." (Proverbs 26:20 NIV) If there is strife in your family or in your workplace, the best thing you can do is to refuse to feed into it with inflammatory, angry, or bitter words.

When we devote our lives to the Lord, He provides us with Christlike believers who we can share some of our secrets with. "A gossip betrays a confidence, but a trustworthy person keeps a secret." (Proverbs 11:13 NIV) We should never share confidential matters with those who are not "trustworthy," or who have a reputation for being gossipers. "A gossip betrays a confidence; so avoid anyone who talks too much." (Proverbs 20:19 NIV) Beware of those who love to hear themselves talk – the ones who crave being the center of attention, and who dominate conversations. This is a sure sign of a lack of self-control, and a warning that these people will eventually give in to the urge to tell others' secrets. Critical speech destroys friendships and divides families, as the woman who wrote me could sadly attest to. "A troublemaker plants seeds of strife; gossip separates the best of friends." (Proverbs 16:28 NLT) Steer clear of those who thrive on creating conflict through bitter words and hurtful behavior.

Without knowing you personally, I can tell you how to have a closer relationship with God, how to have a stronger and happier marriage and family, how to be more successful in your work and ministry, and how to be more prosperous financially. Become a more merciful person. Resist the inclination to criticize others. Walk in forgiveness. Refuse to hold anything against anyone. Sounds like a tall order, I know. But if you have trusted Jesus as your Savior, and made Him the Lord of your life, you can put these principles into practice while drawing on the resurrection power of Christ that abides in you. (Ephesians 1:19-20) God is calling you up higher today. Will you answer that call?

Lord, when I am tempted to speak bitterly against anyone, remind me that Your Word says that "loose talk has a way of getting picked up and spread around." When I hear others gossiping, or "planting seeds of strife," help me not to feed into their sinful behavior. Please provide me with godly, trustworthy friends who I can confide in when Your Spirit leads me to. Teach me how to avoid people who cannot control their emotions or their speech. Make me a peacemaker, instead of a "troublemaker". Today, I pray according to Your Word – "Set a guard over my mouth, O Lord; keep watch over the door of my lips"! (Ecclesiastes 10:10 MSG; Proverbs 16:28; Psalm 141:3 NIV)

Promise-Power Point: *If I will refrain from critical speech, gossip, and strife, I will not have to suffer the bitter consequences of these things, and I will position myself to be richly blessed in my relationships, my work, my ministry, and my finances.*

When the Wicked Succeed

"Be still before the Lord and wait patiently for Him; do not fret when people succeed in their ways, when they carry out their wicked schemes." Psalm 37:7 NIV

Through my ministry, I regularly hear from Christians who suffer injustices at the hands of wicked people, and who are left bewildered, disheartened, and even angry. They ask for prayer and advice, and many times, they want an explanation. My own husband, Joe, felt like this not long ago when a dear friend of his suddenly cut him out of her will right before she died. For decades, Joe had been like a son to this woman, even when she had alienated all of her other friends by her hurtful behavior. She had no family, so my husband took on the responsibility of giving her sound advice, looking out for her interests, and protecting her from those who he thought were taking advantage of her. This lady confessed to Joe that she had included him in her will because he had been there for her when no one else was.

When my husband switched jobs, and was no longer working near this lady's home, he kept in touch with her by phone, and did his best to continue to advise and counsel her. When she became deathly ill, a stranger offered to take care of her dog while she was hospitalized. This man quickly took over her finances, and convinced her to change her will, leaving her money to him in payment for his time and attention.

After she passed away, and it was discovered that she left her estate to this stranger, the police got involved because the situation seemed so suspicious, and they questioned Joe to see what he thought of the whole matter. Joe told them honestly that he didn't know the stranger personally, and that he had no proof that the man did anything wrong. My husband confessed to me that he was hurt and bewildered by his friend's decision to cut him out of her will so abruptly just before she died. He said that he never knew what she intended to leave him, but that even if it had been a very small thing, her remembrance of him in such a kind way would show just how much she appreciated all that he had done for her all those years.

King Solomon wrote, "The blessing of the Lord makes one rich, and He adds no sorrow with it." (Proverbs 10:22 NKJV) I told my husband that perhaps God prevented him from receiving an inheritance from his friend because He knew that it would only bring him trouble and grief. No one knew better than the Lord how all those years Joe had cared for his friend and looked out for her interests. So I truly believe that God was keeping His promise to my husband to work all things together for his good, when He did not protect and send forth his inheritance from this lady. (Romans 8:28) Perhaps it was a test that the Lord felt Joe needed to pass. Scripture says that God "will bring to light what is hidden in darkness and will expose the motives of the heart." (1 Corinthians 4:5 NIV) I told Joe that if he had looked out for his friend all those years with the right motives, then he wouldn't have expected any kind of reward for his good deeds. He agreed with me, and it led him to do some serious soul-searching.

God's Word makes it clear that He doesn't want His children grasping for things that are not His best for them. Proverbs says, "Better to be lowly in spirit along with the oppressed than to share plunder with the proud." (Proverbs 16:19 NIV) In other words, the Lord would rather have us oppressed and among the humble, than prospering with the proud. A passage in the Gospel of Luke gives us an idea of how Jesus felt about this subject. "Then someone called from the crowd, 'Teacher, please tell my brother to divide our father's estate with me.' Jesus replied, 'Friend, who made me a judge over you to decide such things as that?' Then He said, 'Beware! Guard against every kind of greed. Life is not measured by how much you own.'" (Luke 12:13-15 NLT) There are many kinds of greed, and the Master is telling us to guard ourselves against all of them. When we start feeling that someone owes us something to the point that we lose our peace or joy, then we have a heart and attitude problem, and we need to confess it to God and ask for His forgiveness. Otherwise, we will live in bondage to our emotions and feelings, and it will affect our health, our peace of mind, and even our relationship with the Lord.

When it seems like wicked people are getting the best of us, the Bible has some wise counsel for us. "Be still before the LORD and wait patiently for Him; do not fret when people succeed in their ways, when they carry out their wicked schemes." (Psalm 37:7 NIV) God doesn't want us fretting and fuming about those who seem to be triumphing over His people. He wants us to trust Him, and to commit the matter to Him, believing that He is a just God, and that absolutely "nothing is hidden from His sight". (Hebrews 4:13 NIV) This Psalm goes on to say: "The wicked plot against the godly; they snarl at them in defiance. But the Lord just laughs, for He sees their day of judgment coming." (Psalm 37:12-13 NLT) The fact is that no one is getting away with anything for very long. God will indeed judge those who violate His laws, especially those who come against His faithful ones. If you don't believe that, you will spend your life trying to get justice for yourself and your loved ones, and all you will accomplish is to delay or prevent the Lord from acting on your behalf. Today, let us make a quality decision not to "set [our] hopes on uncertain riches, but on God, Who richly and ceaselessly provides us with everything for [our] enjoyment"! (1 Timothy 6:17 AMP)

Lord, I ask that You work in my heart so that whenever I face injustice of any kind, I will respond in a Christlike manner. Cleanse me of every kind of greed, covetousness, and envy. Help me to commit all of my conflicts and battles to You, and to cooperate with You every step of the way, so that I can receive the victories that You have in store for Your devoted and faithful ones. When others seem to succeed in their wicked schemes, remind me that You are ultimately in control, and that You will work all things together for my good when I put my wholehearted trust in You. Thank You that You are not a stingy God, but a generous One "who piles on all the riches we could ever manage"! (1 Timothy 6:17 MSG)

Promise-Powered Point: I may suffer some temporary injustices in this life, but if I will refuse to doubt God, and commit my battles and circumstances to Him, I will ultimately see Him transform all of my troubles into triumphs for His glory.

A God Who Works Behind the Scenes

"While the harpist was playing, the hand of the LORD came on Elisha and he said, 'This is what the LORD says: I will fill this valley with pools of water. For this is what the LORD says: You will see neither wind nor rain, yet this valley will be filled with water, and you, your cattle and your other animals will drink. This is an easy thing in the eyes of the LORD; He will also deliver Moab into your hands.'" 2 Kings 3:15-18 NIV

In the Second Book of Kings in the Bible, there is a fascinating account of how God sometimes chooses to demonstrate His power on behalf of His people without any warning or outward signs. The kings of Israel, Judah, and Edom had united to attack Moab. After a seven-day march, the army had no water left for themselves or their animals. Their situation looked hopeless, and they were prepared to die. Then good King Jehoshaphat summoned Elisha, the prophet of God, who revealed the Lord's plan to perform a miracle on their behalf. To me, the most amazing part of this prophecy is the Lord saying, "You will see neither wind nor rain..." God is saying here, "You're not going to see any signs that a miracle is coming, but it's coming just the same." And not only was God going to do something that was virtually impossible, but He said, "This is an EASY thing in the eyes of the Lord."

I can think of so many times that I encountered challenges in my life, and though a part of me hoped that God would intervene on my behalf, my faith faltered because I thought, "I don't see any signs that He's doing anything!" The fleshly part of me wanted to see something tangible, although the spiritual part of me knew that God was perfectly capable of working wonders on my behalf without any visible signs. The great prophet of God, Isaiah, declared, "Clearly, You are a God who works behind the scenes." (Isaiah 45:15 MSG) That's one reason why the apostle Paul stated, "We live by believing and not by seeing." (2 Corinthians 5:7 NLT)

Are you waiting to see some evidence that God is working on your behalf in a situation? Are you waiting for the right phone call, letter in the mail, or other tangible evidence? Rest assured that it is an easy thing for God to come to your aid, even when signs that He will do so are virtually nonexistent!

Lord, forgive me when I have doubted You because I couldn't see any signs that You had plans to help me. Remind me that Your power and wisdom transcend my comprehension, and that Your love for me knows no bounds. Teach me how to "walk by faith, and not by sight," as Your Word declares. (2 Corinthians 5:7 NKJV) Help me to cooperate with You for the building of my faith by devoting myself to prayer and Scripture study. Thank You that my breakthrough is on its way right now – with or without signs!

Promise-Power Point: When I truly believe that God can work behind the scenes without any outward signs, I will be able to wait on Him with peace and joy in my heart.

High Quality Companionship

"Oh, the joys of those who do not follow evil men's advice, who do not hang around with sinners, scoffing at the things of God. But they delight in doing everything God wants them to, and day and night are always meditating on His laws and thinking about ways to follow Him more closely. They are like trees along a riverbank bearing luscious fruit each season without fail. Their leaves shall never wither and all they do shall prosper." Psalm 1:1-3 TLB

My husband, Joe, and I were grocery shopping the other night when we ran into a lady who used to be the greeter at a department store we shop at regularly. This woman, whom I will call Mabel, had taken time off from work to have some major surgery done. When we saw her that evening, she told us that she had lost her job because she waited too long to go back to work after her recuperation. Mabel was a Christian, but she admitted that she was struggling in her faith because of the people around her who were constantly telling her what they thought she should do. All of them seemed convinced that they had the right solution to her problems, and they bombarded her relentlessly with their counsel and advice. As she went into great detail about the people she surrounded herself with, Mabel revealed that one of her closest friends was trying to rob her and put her confidential information online. Another friend of hers had taken her to a church where the pastor and congregation were practicing witchcraft. And one of her siblings called her regularly with "words from the Lord" that she knew in her heart were lies of the devil. As she spoke, Mabel confessed that she was suffering from anxiety and depression, and that all she wanted was some peace. She wished that everyone would stop trying to run her life, and she said that perhaps it was better for her to be alone.

As I listened to Mabel lament about her problems, and her lack of peace, I realized what one of her biggest problems was. While she was waiting on God for a breakthrough in her job situation, she was unwisely subjecting herself to bossy, disobedient people who were giving her poor advice, and causing her to become fearful and doubtful. She had forgotten the Lord's admonition which says, "The righteous should choose his friends carefully, for the way of the wicked leads them astray." (Proverbs 12:26 NKJV) I encounter good Christian people on a regular basis who naively believe that the people they associate with are not going to lead them astray. They know that the Bible clearly warns us about the quality of our relationships, but they seem to have the notion that theirs will be the exception to the rule. And it profoundly affects their lives in countless ways. Scripture warns: "Guard your heart above all else, for it determines the course of your life." (Proverbs 4:23 NLT) We are the only ones who can guard our hearts. Others can't do it for us. And God won't do it for us.

The apostle Paul wrote: "God wants His children to live in peace." (1 Corinthians 7:15 NLT) One of the reasons why Jesus went to the Cross was so that He could secure peace for us in a dark and cold world. "I am leaving you with a gift – peace of mind and heart. And the peace I give isn't like the peace the world gives. So don't be troubled or afraid." (John 14:27 NLT) Christ's peace is our blood-bought inheritance, but we can relinquish that peace when we surround ourselves with negative people who don't have our best interests at heart, and who continually spout words of doubt and unbelief.

The Bible reveals that God has excellent and extraordinary plans for the lives of all of His children. "For we are God's [own] handiwork (His workmanship), recreated in Christ Jesus, [born anew] that we may do those good works which God predestined (planned beforehand) for us [taking paths which He prepared ahead of time], that we should walk in them [living the good life which He prearranged and made ready for us to live]." (Ephesians 2:10 AMP) But there are opposing forces operating in this world that are committed to preventing us from "living the good life" which the Lord has in store for us. The apostle Peter makes it clear who those forces are when he writes: "Be well balanced (temperate, sober of mind), be vigilant and cautious at all times; for that enemy of yours, the devil, roams around like a lion roaring [in fierce hunger], seeking someone to seize upon and devour." (1 Peter 5:8 AMP) One of the ways that Satan is able to exercise a certain amount of influence over our lives is to do his best to surround us with people who would get us out of God's will. If we are not careful, we can unwittingly cooperate with the devil's evil plans for us, rather than God's good plans for us.

So what kind of companions are we to surround ourselves with if we are going to experience God's best? Scripture advises, "Enjoy the companionship of those who call on the Lord with pure hearts." (2 Timothy 2:22 NLT) This sounds like a tall order, I know. But I have discovered that when we allow God to choose who we spend our time with, He delights in sending us high-quality companions who will love us with His kind of love, and who will pray for us, and believe God for us, even when the odds are stacked against us. The psalmist wisely declares, "I am a companion of all those who fear You, and of those who keep Your precepts." (Psalm 119:63 NASB) If you don't have genuine God-fearing friends and loved ones to support you in hard times, then don't stop praying for them until the Lord sends them. Be prepared to endure seasons of loneliness, if necessary, to receive this precious gift. The best things in life are worth waiting for.

Don't allow listening to the wrong voices to cause you to miss out on God's good plans for you. Voices like these can confuse you, and cause you to lose your sense of direction, as well as your peace. Choose to be alone rather than to spend time with people who discourage you, or who try to get your focus off of God. The kind of companions that God provides will always point you to Him, His ways, His wisdom, and His Word. And never forget the Savior's promise: "And be sure of this – that I am with you always, even to the end of the world." (Matthew 28:20 TLB)

Lord, Your Word says, "become wise by walking with the wise; hang out with fools and watch your life fall to pieces." (Proverbs 13:20 MSG) Please teach me how to avoid associating with "fools," and how to seek out wise, God-fearing people. I long to have the kind of relationships that will help me to live the "good life" You've called me to. Enable me to do whatever it is I need to do to receive relationships like these from You. Send me people who will love me with Your kind of love, and teach me to love them the same way. Grant me friends and loved ones who will encourage my devotion to You, and who will inspire me to fulfill my God-given purpose and potential. Thank You that as I obey You in these areas, I won't have to miss out on any of the best and brightest plans You have for me!

Promise-Power Point: As I believe that God is good, and has good plans for my life, and as I cooperate with Him to surround myself with God-fearing and God-honoring people, I will reap all the blessings, rewards, and opportunities that He has in store for me.

God Will Do a Strange Thing

"[The Lord] will come to do a strange thing; He will come to do an unusual deed." Isaiah 28:21 NLT

I had my Oldsmobile Cutlass for 22 years, when it began breaking down so often that I no longer felt safe driving it. For years, I had been praying and believing God to provide me with a more reliable car, but my husband, Joe, and I were still not in a position to replace it anytime soon. Once again, I called on the Lord to consider my plight, and to act on my behalf somehow. I asked Him to cause my husband to sympathize with my situation so much, that he would be moved to offer me some real help. We talked about buying a new car, and we prayed about it, but we knew in our hearts that it would just put us deeper into debt.

Then, it became obvious to me that God was really working in my husband's heart for my sake. Joe told me, "From now on, I will take your car to work, and you can drive MY car!" After getting over the initial shock, I told my husband that I would give it a try. Suddenly, instead of driving a 22-year-old car, I was driving a 3-year-old car every day. To top it off, my old car never gave my husband a bit of trouble, but always performed perfectly, until he was able to purchase himself a new car.

The Scripture says: "[God] will come to do a strange thing; He will come to do an unusual deed." (Isaiah 28:21 NLT) I've discovered that when you ask the Lord to come to your aid, He may surprise you by doing something totally unexpected and unusual. In my case, I never in my wildest dreams expected my husband to offer me his own car. He was always saying how much he loved driving it, and what a pleasure it was to drive it to work every day. It never occurred to me that he would consider giving it up to drive a 22-year-old vehicle that would be an embarrassment for him to drive to work. Nevertheless, after God put it on his heart to trade cars with me, Joe cheerfully sacrificed his favorite vehicle, and the Lord rewarded him by not only making my old car work perfectly for him, but by enabling him to purchase a beautiful new car for himself two years later – at an extraordinary price!

One of the problems we have when we are faced with adversity or challenging situations of some kind, is that we limit God because we can't envision a desirable solution. Many times, the Lord wants to do "a strange thing" or "an unusual deed," but our lack of faith and vision prevent Him. So I say to you today – whatever need you have at this moment, God has a creative, custom-made solution to your problem. Call on Him right now, and open the door for Him to do something strange and wonderful on your behalf!

Lord, I praise You for being such a creative genius, as well as a generous and gracious God. I thank You that even when it seems like there is no hope for me or my situation, You already have a tailor-made solution for me. Please expand my vision and enable me to trust You for the "impossible". Help me to have the kind of relationship with You that would allow You to work wonders on my behalf on a regular basis. Today, I commit myself to expect the unexpected from You every day!

Promise-Power Point: God longs to perform strange and unusual deeds on my behalf, and I will see Him do exactly that when I work with Him to build my faith and expand my vision – and to pray for the extraordinary.

Painful Times

"This third I will bring into the fire; I will refine them like silver and test them like gold. They will call on my name and I will answer them; I will say, 'They are my people,' and they will say, 'The Lord is our God.'"
Zechariah 13:9 NIV

I have been through many trials when the Lord has used the passage above to speak to my heart. It has been God's way of assuring me that He has a divine purpose for my suffering that will ultimately work for my good. I must confess that when I see any form of the word "refine" in the Scriptures, it makes me shudder. I know that it often refers to the process of refining precious metals, which involves heating the metals until all impurities have been removed. I once heard someone say that God may not change our circumstances until our circumstances change us. So I have found it very valuable to seek the Lord during troubled times to find out what it is He wants me to learn from my distress. Since God can control the intensity and duration of my trials, I count on Him to protect and reward me as I make a quality decision to cooperate with His desires and purposes for them.

What fills me with hope when I read Zechariah 13:9 is the part that says, "They will call on My name and I will answer them; I will say, 'They are My people,' and they will say, 'The Lord is our God.'" In other words, for those of us who belong to the Lord, our suffering is meant to draw us closer to Him, and to enable us to get ready answers to our prayers. The Message Bible puts it this way – "Then they'll pray to Me by name and I'll answer them personally."

A similar passage in the Scriptures is Psalm 66:10-12 (NKJV): "For You, O God, have tested us; You have refined us as silver is refined. You brought us into the net; You laid affliction on our backs. You have caused men to ride over our heads; We went through fire and through water; but You brought us out to rich fulfillment." These verses speak of the intense suffering God allowed His people to go through in order to "test" and "refine" them. The saddest part for me is where the psalmist declares, "You have caused men to ride over our heads." The Amplified translation adds, "when we were prostrate". That tells me that there are times when the Lord will allow people to kick us when we are down. When these people are the ones who are supposed to love us the most, it can be especially painful.

Fortunately, that is not the end of the story. After testing and refining us, the Lord "brings us out" of our misery. He never meant for us to stay in a painful place, but to only allow us to pass through it. Sure, we can camp there if we want to, by prolonging our trials more than necessary. How do we do that? By failing to seek God's wisdom, comfort, and healing in the midst of them. By focusing too much on our misery, and drowning ourselves in self-pity, bitterness, and resentment. By lashing out at others and mistreating them, instead of keeping our "love walk" intact. Or by playing the "blame game" and refusing to see the part that we played in our own problems. On the other hand, as we keep our eyes on the Lord, and ask for and receive His guidance, consolation, and strength, He will "bring us out to rich fulfillment" – even the fulfillment of our fondest hopes and dreams.

Both of these passages assure us that when God allows us to go through painful times, He always has good intentions and purposes in mind for us. If you will believe that and remember that when you are hurting, you will never lose hope, no matter how intense your trials get. How can YOU apply the truths in this message to YOUR life today?

Lord, when You allow me to pass through refining fires, remind me that You always have good purposes for them. Lead me to seek Your wisdom, power, and comfort in difficult times. Help me to hear and to heed Your voice every step of the way. Don't allow me to wallow in self-pity, resentment, or bitterness. Teach me to cooperate with You every moment so that I won't unintentionally intensify or prolong my trials. Thank You that because of Your goodness and mercy, my troubles will draw me closer to You, and to the fulfillment of my hopes and dreams!

Promise-Power Point: As I respond wisely to my trials with God's help, He will cause me to emerge from them better than ever before in every way, and I will enjoy a closer relationship with Him, as well as the realization of my fondest desires and dreams.

How God Speaks to Us

"My sheep hear My voice, and I know them, and they follow Me." John 10:27 NKJV

I often hear from people who ask me how they can hear from God. I tell them that God's will for them is knowable and doable, and that the Lord is eager to communicate with His children. When we do our part in the communication process, we always discover that God is faithful to do His.

First, God speaks to us through His Word. Scripture says, "Your word is a lamp to guide my feet and a light for my path." (Psalm 119:105 NLT) What is your greatest need today? Does it have to do with your finances, your relationships, your work, or your health? Whatever it is, if you will approach the Lord with an open Bible, and ask Him to speak to your heart about your need, He will lead you to Scriptures that will address your concerns. As you apply the principles contained in those verses, you will see doors open and mountains move. It may not happen overnight, but it will happen, because God's Word – His Truth – never fails. God's Word works, when we put it to work.

The Lord also speaks to us through His Holy Spirit. Jesus said: "Everything that the Father has is Mine. That is what I meant when I said that He [the Spirit] will take the things that are Mine and will reveal (declare, disclose, transmit) it to you." (John 16:15 AMP) Like a heavenly transmitter, the Holy Spirit will bring us revelation from heaven that will enable us to live lives of victory and abundance – lives that honor God. One way that we can recognize instruction from the Spirit, is that it is in harmony with the Word of God. If what we hear contradicts the principles of Scripture, we can be sure that it is not from God, but from our own carnal minds or the evil one, Satan. I often like to pray, "Lord, make me sensitive and obedient to Your Spirit's leading in these matters."

The Lord can even use our circumstances to speak to us. The Bible says: "The steps of a [good] man are directed and established by the Lord when He delights in his way [and He busies Himself with his every step]." (Psalm 37:23 AMP) In other words, when we are committed to living for God and seeking His will, He will direct our steps and order our circumstances for our good and His glory. Suppose you are looking for a job. As you earnestly pray for God's best in the situation, you can ask Him to shut every door against you but the right one. As you continue to stand in faith for the answer, you can trust that the Lord will use your circumstances to guide you to the job that is right for you in His sight. Even if you make a mistake, it's not the end of the world, because God is on your side. As the following verse states: "Though he falls, he shall not be utterly cast down, for the Lord grasps his hand in support and upholds him." (Psalm 37:24 AMP)

God often uses our relationships to speak to us. This is why the quality of our relationships is so important in God's sight, and should be in our own. Scripture says: "The godly offer good counsel; they teach right from wrong. They have made God's law their own, so they will never slip from His path." (Psalm 37:30-31 NLT) A Christian who is living a life of obedience can be one of the greatest assets to our walk with God. If we are having trouble hearing from the Lord in a certain area, we can ask Him to use a godly companion of ours to give us clarification and confirmation. However, we are not to depend on other people to hear from God for us; we are to depend only upon the Holy Spirit. But God can, and does, use others when it suits His purposes to do so.

Jesus said: "My sheep hear My voice, and I know them, and they follow Me." (John 10:27 NKJV) You already have everything you need to hear from God. Take a moment and call on Him today. He longs to speak to you.

Lord, help me to devote myself to Your Word, so that You can use it to impart Your perfect wisdom to me. Teach me to be sensitive and obedient to the voice of Your Spirit. Shut against me all the wrong doors, and open wide before me all the right doors. Grant me God-honoring relationships that will benefit me spiritually. Thank You for directing my steps in paths of victory and success, as I live my life for You!

Promise-Power Point: God has specific and unique purposes and plans for my life, and His will for me is knowable and doable. And as I walk in close fellowship with Him throughout each day – keeping an open heart and willing mind – He will guide and guard my steps so that I don't miss out on His best for me.

About the Author

Since 1998, **J. M. Farro** has served as the devotional writer and prayer counselor for Jesusfreakhideout.com – one of the first and largest Christian music web sites in the world. Her mission is to help others to discover the life-changing power of having a deeply personal relationship with Christ.

Through devotionals, podcasts, blogs, and books – including the best-selling *Life on Purpose* devotional book series – she encourages others to fulfill their God-given purpose and potential. She and her husband, Joe, have two sons, and live in Nazareth, Pennsylvania.

J. M. Farro
Nazareth, PA 18064

jmf@jmfarro.com
farro@jesusfreakhideout.com

www.jmfarro.com
www.jesusfreakhideout.com
www.littlejesusfreaks.com

Other J. M. Farro Books in This Series

The Promise-Powered Life

The Promise-Powered Life for Women

The Promise-Powered Life for Men

The Promise-Powered Life for Parents

NOTES

Made in the USA
Lexington, KY
09 June 2016